The Christian Man's Guide to Spiritual Self-Defense

The Christian Man's Guide to Spiritual Self-Defense

Understanding the Lord God's Communication
about the *Real* Holy Warrior in You

Patrick L. Stearns

Foreword by Mike Markham

RESOURCE *Publications* · Eugene, Oregon

THE CHRISTIAN MAN'S GUIDE TO SPIRITUAL SELF-DEFENSE
Understanding the Lord God's Communication about the Real Holy Warrior in You

Resource Publications
An Imprint of Wipf and Stock Publishers
199 W. 8th Ave., Suite 3
Eugene, OR 97401

www.wipfandstock.com

PAPERBACK ISBN: 978-1-5326-8352-7
HARDCOVER ISBN: 978-1-5326-8353-4
EBOOK ISBN: 978-1-5326-8354-1

Manufactured in the U.S.A.   JANUARY 8, 2020

This work is dedicated to the Lord God, my Father, Jesus Christ, my Lord and Savior, and the guidance of the Holy Spirit. I also thank my awesome gift from the Lord God, my lovely wife, Karen, and my parents, Clyde and Martha Stearns. I thank the Lord God Almighty for you every day. Finally, I want to thank Stephen and Tina Johnson. The Triune God worked through you to inspire me to write this book. I am humbly and eternally grateful that you are treasured family in the body of Christ for Karen and me. I would also like to thank Dr. Belinda Wheeler and Dr. Richard Brown for guiding me through the crucial parts, regarding key understanding of the process. I appreciate your experience and guidance. Finally, I would like to thank Mr. Anthony Reed, one of my key life's mentors.

Contents

Foreword

THE CHRISTIAN MAN'S GUIDE to *Spiritual Self-Defense* is essential reading for any Christian man who seeks to be more than just an average Christian and more than just an average man. While we are all aware of our past and current shortcomings—sometimes painfully so—no one truly desires to be average. Certainly, the God who created us doesn't desire for his treasured creations to languish in mediocrity. This book helps, guides, and encourages the Christian man to take up his true responsibilities and make appropriate decisions that lead to personal growth that will benefit him and those around him.

Author Patrick Stearns has an easy, straightforward, and loving communication style. He is a professional communicator and has allowed God to use that gift. You can feel God's love and guidance coming through the words he has penned. In a society that is increasingly dismissive of and hostile towards the concept of masculinity, Stearns presents clear and understandable biblical truths on how God expects men to conduct themselves. However, this book is not meant to condemn men or make us feel the shame of our past mistakes or current shortcomings. It is designed to positively and lovingly guide and instruct us through a process and down a path of greater responsibility, maturity, and fulfillment. It encourages and guides us to live a life better than the one we may have previously lived and better than the one we may have had modeled to us in our youth. And it certainly lights the path to living a life better than the often confusing and inappropriate one that is encouraged and normalized through media and popular culture.

Men need help, encouragement, and guidance. This book offers all of those things through biblical truth and practical examples. The author should also be commended for his candor regarding his own past mistakes. We all have a past and not all of that past is positive. Thankfully, our God forgives and forgets our sins and gives us an opportunity move forward in a positive way every moment of every day. *The Christian Man's Guide to Spiritual Self-Defense* will help men practically move forward in love, positivity, and maturity.

Enjoy the pages of this book and all it has to offer. Allow God to speak to you and help you to be a more fulfilled, more effective, and more confident man through his perfect and loving ways. Allow God, with the help of Patrick Stearns, to guide you into a more positive and fulfilling life. A life that honors him, blesses you, and benefits those you love and the world and community in which you live.

—Mike Markham
   Globally-Recognized Olympics, Pan American Games, Boxing and Mixed Martial Arts Broadcast and Ring Announcer

Introduction

Why Spiritual Self-Defense?

BROTHERS IN CHRIST, WE need *spiritual self-defense*. History shows that every great modern movement we in the body of Christ have engaged in has always had some kind of spiritual center. We have always, as Christians, looked to the Trinity—the Lord God the Father, the Lord God the Son, and the Lord God the Holy Spirit—to successfully achieve progress in the United States, and other parts of the world. Many of our organizations have a Lord God-centered foundation. We can look at our colleges and universities, civil rights organizations, and fraternal organizations and find that the foundation is one centered upon Christian principles.

I believe when we, as Christian men, follow the Lord God-centered instruction, we succeed in anything we do, as long as it is good in the eyes of the Lord. We fail when we lean unto our own understanding, and try to do it our own way. We must do what the Lord God would have us do. When we do this, we are practicing true wisdom; a key part of spiritual self-defense. The Bible tells us to love wisdom (Prov 4:6). History shows that our greatest Christian leaders did this, and we must follow their example. Spiritual self-defense makes sense because is constitutes wisdom in the body of Christ.

But what exactly is spiritual self-defense? It is praying and reading your Bible regularly, going to a Bible-teaching, Bible-believing church, and seeking the guidance of the Lord God, his Son Jesus, and the Holy Spirit. This is your armor. This is your sword and shield. This is your fortress. You need all of this to combat an enemy who is already defeated, but is too stupid and too full of lies and deceit to have enough sense to realize it. Make no mistake, brothers; Satan, although he is a defeated, underhanded, murderous liar, is always busy. Yet he only has some power. Our Lord God is omnipotent, and has power over all. Satan cannot be everywhere all the time, so he has to use demons to work through people (who usually don't realize they're being used in the first place). Our the Lord God is omnipresent; one who is everywhere. Your enemy, Satan, only knows so much Therefore he uses lies, deception, and confusion as his specialty, in order to make up for his lack of knowledge. Even if he were smarter than he is, he would use it against you anyway. Our the Lord God is omniscient; he knows all and is the Father of Knowledge.

So, you are going to have to be a black belt in spiritual self-defense if you want to come out of these battles on two feet. Make no mistake, my brothers; we are at war. Satan wants us to live every kind of lifestyle contrary to the Lord God's plan. He wants us to be addicted to legal and illegal drugs in order to stifle our being the community warriors of change that the Lord God has commissioned us to be. He wants us to make horrible decisions that break up our families so we will not be in the home loving our wives. He does not want us to raise our children, so they can grow up to be undisciplined and unproductive citizens who turn around and perpetuate a vicious cycle of irresponsibility in all its apathetic, nonproductive ways. We need to break this cycle, and spiritual self-defense is the key. Brothers, we were not put on this earth to be spiritual wimps. We are of a royal priesthood; the Bible tells us so (1 Pet 2:9). We must learn how to take our rightful place as effective leaders and productive members in our community and in the body of Christ. Learn spiritual self-defense, and brother, you will be well on your way. It's time to get you "strapped" spiritually. Get ready, brothers, because, when it comes to dealing with the enemy, it's time for you to learn about the weapons for your warfare.

Chapter 1

Bible Study

Understanding That Your Best Line
of Defense Is Your Offense

I DO MY BEST to remember to have my Bible nearby; my office, my car, and other strategic places. I know that once I leave my house (after being prayed up, of course), for every situation I encounter, be it one with racist overtones, for example, or dealing with someone who is struggling with low self-esteem and wants to start some stuff with me out in the street, or my job (or even in the church!), and other places, I must always have the Lord God's word as a reference. At the very least, I usually have my Bible packed in my book bag, or strategically situated on or near my car's passenger seat; a great way of making sure I read it anytime I have a moment, no matter where I am. I use that book bag for work and research. The Bible is the most important book in that book bag. As a matter of fact, it is the most important book I own. Brothers, I want you to understand this: as men living in this society, your knowing and applying what the Bible says about you will guide you through any situation.

First, you'll have to know where to start. When I began this journey, the Lord God blessed me with pastoral mentorship, regarding where I should begin reading the word. I did not have a clue where to start. It was January 1988. I had moved to Washington, DC, to begin graduate studies at Howard University. I had moved from Glendale, Ohio, a town sixteen miles north of Cincinnati. I had moved from a village of about 2,500 people to the big city, and I felt overwhelmed. I had to adjust to a new way of living, for I had never lived in a city, much less interacted with people from an urban area. The fast pace, the unfriendliness of so many people, the gunshots and ambulance sirens at night, and many other similar occurrences resulted in my needing to remain tied in spiritually. I found a church home, St. Paul's AME Church, where the Reverend Henry Y. White was the pastor. Every Wednesday night, I especially looked forward to the Bible study. I knew that I was going to receive more spiritual food to help get me through the rest of the week, and by Sunday, I would receive more nourishment. The Lord God had placed Rev. White and the other saints at St. Paul AME in my life to not only help me make it through my experiences in the city, but to also remind me of who I am and whose I am. They, especially Reverend White, reminded me of the importance of always staying spiritually connected, and continually working on my spiritual self-defense.

I thank the Lord God that he had already been beginning the process of preparing me for spiritual self-defense before I had even left home. Before arriving to Washington, DC, I had left Glendale to pursue undergraduate studies at Ohio University. The pastor at my first church home, Bethel AME Church in Lockland, Ohio, the Reverend Earl Harris, had encouraged me to read the book of Proverbs daily. He explained to me that just as King Solomon had instructed his son with advice for successful living in this book, this same text would instruct me, too. I read the book regularly when I was at school, and it helped me deal with situations that would have gotten me into trouble had I dealt with them my own way instead of the Lord God's way. While at undergraduate and graduate school, for example, I rarely got into arguments or any real contentious conflicts with anybody. This was the case because I saw where the Bible instructed me not to get into any needless arguments (2 Tim 2:23). In addition, I remember the book of

Proverbs stating that "it is to one's honor to avoid strife, but every fool is quick to quarrel" (Prov 20:3). Also, when anyone showed anger toward me, I responded in a calm tone, which would defuse their anger. I had applied, and still continue to apply the scripture "a soft answer turns away wrath, but harsh words cause quarrels" (Prov 15:1). Since 1992, I have been blessed with the calling of being university faculty. I've had various students from all walks of life in my classes. Believe me, although the majority of them over the years have been focused young adults who handle the classroom experience successfully, I have had, and continue to have, students who bring life's difficulties into the classroom environment. Combine that with a still-developing part of their brain that controls emotions, and one will be in a situation in which one must diffuse inappropriate responses to everything from grade disputes to in-class disruptive behavior. I have received a lot of experience practicing spiritual self-defense in this environment alone! Now this is just one of the examples, yet you must understand that you must be alert constantly, regarding making sure you apply spiritual self-defense.

What do I consider the first point of attack for successfully applying spiritual self-defense? You have heard the saying that the best defense is a good offense, haven't you? Well, that's exactly the way you must apply spiritual self-defense throughout your daily Christian walk. In the sixth chapter of the book of Ephesians, the Apostle Paul, in the seventeenth verse, reminds us to take up the "Sword of the Spirit, which is the word of God." I have learned that when it comes to spiritual warfare, an important lesson we must learn is how to properly use our weapons. An effective warrior, a soldier either on the battlefield or preparing to go to one, is aware of the importance of knowing how to effectively use their weapons, especially the most effective one. That weapon could be a rifle, a machine gun, the weapons on their aircraft or ship; their modern-day swords. Our offensive weapon, the word of God, is important because the offensive process of applying scripture and living that application is what places us on the path to be effective practitioners of spiritual self-defense. There is scripture for every situation in which Satan uses someone to veer you away from your destiny as an effective husband, father, brother, coworker, student, etc.; scripture designed for you to use to literally make the enemy and his demons working inside that person actually flee from you, and therefore remove that unknowingly demon-possessed person from you. Applying the direct blueprint of scripture does this. I have literally applied the Sword of the Spirit, which is the word of God, to spiritually cut my way out of Satan and his demons' attempts to trap me. For example the Bible tells us to "submit yourselves therefore to the Lord. Resist the devil and he will flee from you" (James 4:7). If I've ever awaken in the morning, and really did not feel like doing much of anything, I was reminded of the scripture that said, "A wise youth makes hay while the sun shines, but what a shame to see someone waste their hour of opportunity" (Prov 10:5–7). If I am tempted to act in a way that is inconsistent with my Christian walk, I remember 1 Corinthians 10:13, which reminds me that God is so faithful, that when I am tempted, he will show me a way out of the temptation! As a married man, I've been in public places where there have been women who see my wedding ring, and still try to come on to me. The Lord's Prayer reminds me to not be lead into temptation (Matt 6:13). In addition to a happening such as this occurring, spiritual self-defense via the Sword of the Spirit, which is the Word of God, says to me, "You know that this is the enemy trying to tempt you, especially since during your years as a single man, these sorts of things never happened to you around here!" So, I exercise spiritual self-defense by removing myself from the situation; the appropriate action that the scriptures instruct me to do.

Keep in mind that the reason I shared all of the previous information and examples is for this very reason: as the first and very important lesson in spiritual self-defense, since the Bible makes it very clear that the Sword of the Spirit is the word of God, make sure you apply it in every situation. Do this knowing that Satan and his demons are already having a nervous breakdown, knowing that you are studying this tactic, and this already-defeated enemy and his demons will experience a spiritual beatdown by you as long as you apply the word of God in every situation guaranteed to send him and his demons fleeing from you. From the time you wake up, until the time you lay down your head at night, Satan realizes that although he is already defeated and cannot destroy you, he and his demons will stop at nothing to attempt to distract you and slow down your training and development as a child of the Most High God. Therefore, the Bible instructs you to meditate on the word day and night (Joshua 1:8) so that you will *do everything written in it*. Every time I apply this first and most powerful spiritual self-defense tactic, nothing but good results, godly results, take place! It is no coincidence that the Sword of the Spirit is the part of what the Apostle Paul termed putting on the whole armor of God. The other parts of the armor, the helmet of salvation, the breastplate of righteousness, the belt of truth, the shoes of the gospel of peace, the shield of faith, while very important are the defensive parts of the armor. The *only offensive part* is the Sword of the Spirit, which is the word of God (Eph 6:11–17). I strongly encourage you to study this scripture, for your foundation of learning spiritual self-defense is shown there. You must realize that as a child of the Most High God, you have this impregnable defense, followed by an unstoppable offense. This is how spiritual self-defense, your best defense, is your best offense. One cannot work without the other. Just as during the times of antiquity a trained soldier knew how to use his armor in battle, and a modern-day soldier who's trained well knows how to use his or her weapons and equipment for warfare, a successful practitioner of spiritual self-defense knows how to use each and every one of these elements, ensuring that they win their spiritual battles and overall spiritual warfare. Now don't let this be an overwhelming task for you. I encourage you to follow the example of another Christian man who is a leader in the church and who you know is following, living, and applying the word of God. This man could be your pastor or your men's Bible study leader, or just another man in your church, another Bible-teaching, Bible-believing church you know from your community, who you know is applying the Word of God to all areas of his life.

I have found that as I continue to apply the Sword of the Spirit, which is the Word of God, this first step in applying the foundation of spiritual self-defense is something I do my best to remember to apply in every waking moment of my life. Have I always followed these and other scriptures? Not even by a long shot. There have been times when I chose to be hard-headed and do it my own way, and the results were always bad ones. Still, I got up, dusted myself off, and learned the greatest lesson of spiritual self-defense: don't go by your own understanding; always seek the Lord God first, and he will direct your paths (Matt 6:33). Remember my mentioning the importance of loving wisdom (Prov 4:6–7). I have actually read translations of this scripture that say you should love wisdom and common sense. Therefore, it's also just good ol' plain common sense to love wisdom, knowing that the Bible says you will achieve great results upon doing this.

A great example of the application of these spiritual self-defense principles is pastor and recording artist Canton Jones's gospel music song "Stay Saved." Brother Jones encounters a series of situations where, if he handles it the world's way, things will not turn out right. Realizing this, he handles things the Lord God's way by using spiritual self-defense. First, he and his wife are at a show, where a group of misguided young men breaks in the line in front of them. Pastor Jones brings it to the brother's attention, who begins to act as though he wants to fight about it. Brother Jones stays calm, and makes his point that since everybody is going to get a seat, it is not necessary and not right for him to cut in front of others. Brother Jones then tells the misguided brother that he's going to be the bigger man and let the misguided brother stay in line in front of him, because it's not worth getting jumped by the misguided young men or worse. The second scenario depicts Brother Jones at a fast food restaurant where the young lady behind the counter has messed up his order. When Pastor Jones asks her to correct the situation, she refuses to do the right thing, while cursing at the same time. She asks him to go to the back of the line, when not only had he not made the mistake, but on top of things, he is pressed for time. When he asks to see the manager, he finds out that *she's* the manager. He decides not to pursue receiving the correct order or his refund because it is not worth acting outside of the Lord God's will for his life. The verse ends with this great reminder: "You gotta stay prayed up, 'cause folks are gonna test you, she's still cussing, see you later, God bless you, I'm gon' stay saved, aintgon' start fussin', I'm gon' stay saved, aintgon' start cussin', I'm gon' stay saved, even though I'm hot as fire, I'm gon' love you anyhow."

Now here's a young brother in Christ who, when faced with the choice, employs spiritual self-defense. Because of his doing this, he is an anointed pastor, father, and a successful recording artist, whose musical ministry is indicative of being a great work in the Lord. If you want to be successful, you must make the same decisions as Pastor Jones.

I now want to give you your first and most important spiritual defense lesson. I have learned from my mentors in Christ that if you want to be a *real man* in the body of Christ, you must be in *total obedience and submission to the Lord God Almighty.* This first and greatest spiritual self-defense lesson hinges upon your understanding and always following Psalm 128. I learned that every man who really wants to set upon the path of learning and mastering spiritual self-defense must *understand and practice* the instructions contained in Psalm 128.

Let's first read this passage of scripture in its entirety:

> Blessed are all who fear the LORD, who walk in his ways.
> You will eat the fruit of your labor; blessings and prosperity will be yours. Your wife will be like a fruitful vine within your house; your sons will be like olive shoots around your table. Thus is the man blessed who fears the LORD. May the LORD bless you from Zion all the days of your life; may you see the prosperity of Jerusalem, and may you live to see your children's children.

I really want you to study what you're seeing here. I want you to understand that if you want the happiness, joy, success, and freedom that is indicative of really living a worthwhile life, then you absolutely have to understand that this scripture is one of the most important spiritual self-defense tactics that you must practice and master. Let's take a look at verse 1. This verse makes it clear that in order to be blessed, truly blessed, we must learn to and be in full obedience to *all* of the Lord God's ways; not just some. What does this mean? This means that right away, right now, you have to make a decision. You have to decide that you are going to seek the Lord God, regarding everything you do, all areas of your life, and follow his guidelines for your life. Studying this scripture and others is crucial; something that the Bible says you must do frequently (Josh 1:8). This is all about cause and effect. Once you make a decision to do the right thing and follow the Lord God, seeking him first, so that he will direct all you do (again, stressed in Matt 6:33). This is all about getting the relationship right. You are not going to successfully learn and master this spiritual self-defense tactic unless you understand that your relationship with the Lord God is something in which you must be all in. The Bible says that if we're lukewarm or not fully committed to serving the Lord God, he will spit us out (Rev 3:16). I don't know about you, but I want to make sure that my level of spiritual self-defense is at such an acceptable level to the Lord God, that I never want to be in danger of being spat out. I never want to be accused of having a half-stepping commitment that disallows his blessings for me. Remembering the cause-and-effect relationship that we must have with the Lord God reminds us that when we do what we're supposed to do, he blesses us. The book of Deuteronomy makes it clear that the Lord God wants us to have the blessings, and not the curses. There's an entire chapter that talks about this fact (ch. 28). As a matter of fact, you'll find that this chapter emphasizes the cause-and-effect part of establishing a successful relationship with the Lord God that I mentioned previously. This chapter states that if you *fully* obey the Lord God and follow his commandments, he will bless you in everything you do that is good in his sight, and that he will defeat *any* enemy that rises up against you (Deut 28:1–8)! Can't you see how this is an important spiritual self-defense tactic that you *must* master? This is a spiritual self-defense tactic that when mastered, will result in your enemies running away from you!

Verse 7 states that your enemies will come at you from one direction, and flee in *seven different directions*! But just how do we know that this is an effective spiritual self-defense tactic related to the larger practice of spiritual self-defense as a whole? How do we know that when we do the right thing that he blesses us? The Bible says so! Look at Psalm 128, verse 2. It tells us that as long as we work for it, we will receive our just reward; blessings and prosperity! Who doesn't want to be blessed? Who doesn't want to be prosperous? So why should we even entertain the thought of doing things that result in the exact opposite of what the Lord God says he will have for us? If blessings and prosperity are going to be yours, why would you act in such a way or do things that would result in your not receiving these things? Think about this, now!

Using the word as the best defense for your spiritual development, and effective spiritual self-defense is only as good as your reading, understanding, and applying what the word says about your life, and instructs you to do. For example, when engaged in a Muy Thai–influenced self-defense workout, I practice my offense while maintaining a defensive position; poised to throw elbow strikes while keeping my hands near my chin, with my elbows tucked near my ribs. One of the key points the instructors emphasize in all of these self-defense moves is this point: in order for you to successfully keep your opponent or attacker at bay, you must use proper technique. A key part of success for executing an accurate punch, elbow strike, knee, or kick is engaging in proper body rotation. If you don't properly rotate your body, you won't be successful in subduing your opponent or attacker. This is even more important for spiritual self-defense. If you don't apply biblical scripture to every area of your spiritual life, you won't be effective in daily victory over Satan and his demons. The Bible makes it clear that we have already overcome the enemy through standing on the promises of what the Lord God the Father, the Lord God the Son, and the Lord God the Holy Spirit reveals in the scriptures, but we must apply them, meditating on them night and day, and studying them so that we can effectively apply the Word to our lives every day, and win each battle that Satan and his demons wage against us. Remember that once again, the book of Ephesians tells us that the Word of the Lord God is the Sword of the Spirit; the only offensive weapon of the armor of the Lord God. Remember, every other part, the helmet of salvation, the shield of faith, the breastplate of righteousness, the belt of truth, and the shoes of peace, although important, are for defensive purposes. I'm emphasizing this again so that you can get into the habit of practicing this right away. There are going to be times when the process will be frustrating, and you'll probably want to handle situations your way and not the Lord God's way. Remember that it's God, and not you, who are running your life. Every morning, when I wake up, I voice a prayer along the lines in which I say, "Lord God, I arise to do your will." That way, I remind myself to begin the day by always understanding that spiritual self-defense is having the Lord God Almighty take control of every aspect of my life, since he is the one who is always in control. I am just a vessel, a conduit, one who takes spiritual dictation from him. I do what he tells me to do, I have him direct my steps, since my steps are ordered by him anyway. I put on his armor, realizing that he is the most powerful force in the universe, as Pastor Joel Osteen says many times in his sermons. I also pray along those lines before or during the beginning of my morning drive to work. I thank him for who he is; he who is able to keep me from falling, he who gives my wife and pet and me traveling mercies, he who knew me before I was in my mother's womb, and he who is my provider, protector, and peace. I also thank the Lord God Almighty for giving us his son, Jesus, to be the example the world needed and still needs to see. I thank Jesus for being my Lord, Master, and Savior, and for the unimaginable agony that he suffered on Calvary's cross for my sins. I also add to my prayer one of gratitude for Jesus not only dying on that cross, but conquering death, leaving that tomb, rising from that grave, and allowing five hundred believers to see him before he ascended into heaven (see 1 Cor 15:6). I also thank Jesus for leaving the Holy Spirit, the Spirit of Truth, the Comforter, which reminds me to take the high road when I don't feel like it, to "catch a grip" and handle things correctly when I feel flesh rising up, and I'm tempted to do things my way instead of the Lord's way, and for always being my pathfinder for righteousness' sake. I then thank the Triune God, the Holy Trinity, the Father, the Son, and the Holy Spirit, for being that powerful, unbreakable threefold cord that wraps around my marriage and keeps it strong and always growing in him. I always end every prayer in the incomparable, mighty name of Jesus. This is my first daily act of practicing spiritual self-defense. I do this, lest I want to be vulnerable to the attacks of an already-defeated devil. I don't want to ever place myself in that situation, so I'm glad the Lord God has blessed me with this life-saving, life-enhancing spiritual self-defense practice. As long as I realize I have put on the armor of God and know how to use it; that same armor that's covered with the sin-cleansing blood of Jesus, and the guidance of the Holy Spirit, my spiritual self-defense foundation is intact.

At the same time, this doesn't happen without the knowhow, the practice and the self-discipline. In September of 1980, when I was a junior at Princeton High School in Cincinnati, Ohio, Dr. Arthur A. Thomas, president of Central State University in Xenia, Ohio, came to speak to our class; the class of 1982. He said that when it came to positive habits, if we can engage in one for ninety days, we can do it the rest of our lives. I remembered how the Lord worked through Dr. Thomas that day. Since then, I have worked to apply that rule to various aspects of my life. My daily prayer is a key example.

I have found that the process of incorporating good habits and applying a structure such as the ninety-day rule is another spiritually sound commonsense example and habit built upon the belief that the best defense is the best offense. Using the Sword of the Spirit, the awesome word of the Lord, the Lord God, allows me to strike the already-defeated Satan and his demons first. Just correctly quoting, applying, and living by scripture can put anyone whom Satan is using to back off from you. I've used this scripture-based tactic regularly. Believe me; since I'm university faculty, I get a lot of practice! There's either students (usually students) and sometimes fellow colleagues whom the enemy will use to try to push my buttons. The sad part is the fact that many times, they don't even have enough "walking around sense" to realize that Satan is using them in the first place! The word tells us that when we submit to the Lord God Almighty, and resist Satan, our enemy, our defeated adversary, he will flee from us (James 4:7). The point is that in order to effectively use this powerful example of applying the Sword of the Spirit, we must be specific regarding following instructions.

Let's continue to look at this structure. Look at Deuteronomy 28:1–7 as a self-defense move like a specific block-punch-kick or trip-takedown move, and think of the entire chapter of Psalm 128 as the martial art itself. Just as the move is a part of the art, one series of scriptures is related to an entire chapter. Remember that in order to learn spiritual self-defense, you must realize that there are key parts that make up the whole. Learn to apply the Sword of the Spirit, which is the word of God, one scripture at a time, to your actual life occurrences. Do this on a daily basis, and you will realize how every move is connected. Every scripture corresponds to a particular spiritual self-defense tactic or series of tactics. For your own growth in the Lord God's kingdom, seek to understand each one! At one time I practiced the Burmese martial art of Bando. Our instructor always used to talk about muscle memory. He stated the importance of practicing a self-defense move so often that it becomes a reaction that is as automatic as waking up in the morning, or tying our shoes. I once read a short story years ago that described the legendary Samurai Musashi Miyamoto as one who "learned to live on the balls of his feet." I remember reading that his sensei, or instructor, would at times, sneak up on him and whack him with a bamboo sword as he was doing chores; a tactic to get him used to muscle memory, since a seasoned Samurai was always aware of his surroundings to the point of being able to fend off a surprise attack. Years ago, in junior high school, I read this story, so I don't remember the source. However, I do remember the message; one further emphasized during my Bando days at Ohio University.

A few years ago, I witnessed another analogy. I watched a movie about a historic military battle known as the Battle of Red

Cliffs. This battle took place in China during the third century. Two kingdoms had united under an allied force designed to stop a third kingdom that wanted to conquer all of China. The allied forces employed the brilliant military strategist Zhuge Liang. Liang knew that the allied forces were heavily outnumbered, and that their opponent, a powerful warlord by the name of Cao Cao, had a land and naval force of 230,000 men who would soon confront them. Liang devised a strategy in which he first sailed a small fleet of ships in a heavy fog toward Cao Cao's navy. Feigning an attack, each ship had fake dummy "soldiers" standing on each small ship's bow. Cao Cao could not tell that this was a trick, and had his archers fire at the ships. From the safety of the cabins, each ship's captain survived the volley of over one hundred thousand arrows. Liang used the fog to literally collect the arrows, receiving a "donation" of needed ammunition from Cao Cao's army. In addition, Liang prepared fire ships loaded with flammable animal fat, knowing that a southwestern wind was coming during the middle of the afternoon of the day of the battle in the winter of AD 208. The fire ships approached Cao Cao's massive fleet under the false understanding that they were a surrender party. The captains of each ship then set their ships afire, retreating to smaller vessels and sailing back to allied lines. When the southeastern winds fanned the flames of each ship, the results were disastrous for Cao Cao's forces. The fire ships collided with the ships of his forces, setting off a chain reaction similar to a book of matches. Cao Cao had linked his ships from stem to stern to keep his naval soldiers, many who were new to naval warfare, from becoming seasick. Many of Cao Cao's soldiers and horses burned to death. With this massive setback, he had to withdraw and concede defeat. This battle secured the victory for the two allied kingdoms, and saved the southern lands of China from being overrun by Cao Cao's forces.

Here's my point: Zhuge Liang knew that in the midst of overwhelming odds, he relied on something greater than himself to secure victory. He knew that he could rely on the forces of nature, fog and wind, to work to the advantage of an allied force that was outnumbered by several thousand soldiers. My brothers, when we seem overwhelmed by circumstances in our lives, and we realize that in the natural, we are unable to secure a favorable outcome, we can rely on the *supernatural* to work things out for our good. This is also what Psalm 128 is saying to us! This blueprint for our success is making it crystal clear that this most important element of spiritual self-defense is a blueprint for mastering it! Just as Zhuge Liang used the forces of nature to successfully defend the two allied kingdoms, we must use Psalm 128 to successfully *learn and apply* spiritual self-defense!

Brothers, I cannot emphasize enough the importance of knowing, understanding and applying Psalm 128 to your life; a key scripture to beginning the process of mastering spiritual self-defense. I learned the importance of this scripture from Dr. Tony Evans. In his book *Kingdom Man*, he emphasizes the important fact that every Christian man must always apply this scripture, for it is essential to their spiritual success and well-being:

> You become a better man by aligning yourself under the comprehensive rule of the Lord God over every area of your life [Dr. Evans' definition of a kingdom man]. You do it through choosing not just to be a man, but also a *kingdom* man. By being the man that David wrote about in what has become my benchmark passage for manhood, Psalm 128. No other passage in Scripture so comprehensively covers the kingdom impact of a kingdom man through all four spheres of life, which include the personal, family, church, and community. Psalm 128 is specifically written to men to tell them how they are to function. In this once compact yet comprehensive passage, David covers all of the components of a kingdom man in Psalm 128. First and foremost, the blessing comes when a kingdom man fears the Lord and walks in his ways in his personal life.[1]

You have to understand that as you learn this most important spiritual self-defense lesson, you are going to be up against attacks by Satan, your enemy. You must force yourself to repel these attacks by maintaining strong discipline in reading, understanding,

1. Evans, *Kingdom Man*, 145, 146.

and applying this biblical chapter. Satan does not want you to learn spiritual self-defense because he knows that once you do, you will be able to access the most powerful force in the universe against him. He already knows that he is a defeated enemy, and that your oncoming future expertise in spiritual self-defense will hasten his defeat. The enemy will try to distract you with other things in your life, and will do so in order for you not to take the time to learn spiritual self-defense. He will distract you with negative media, unhealthy relationships, and various activities that not only are an extremely poor and unproductive use of your time; they have absolutely nothing to do with advancing the Lord God's kingdom. This is a trap in which you must not enter. You must discipline yourself to stick to your spiritual self-defense training because the spiritual success of you and your family depends on it!

In saying that, an important spiritual self-defense element consists of examining and understanding Psalm 128. Verse 3 makes it clear that as long as we practice spiritual self-defense, mastering this important lesson, it will be positively contagious, enhancing our wives' and children's spiritual growth as well. This is quite revealing because it applies to all Christian men, regardless of their present marital status. Upon mastering the spiritual self-defense lesson of Psalm 128, a man's wife and child or children will grow spiritually as a result of the man's example. At the same time, when a Christian man who is not married and childless does the same thing, he will experience the same results when he does find a saved wife and the two bring children into the world. So therefore, in both examples, the Christian man who masters this foundational biblical chapter, masters a major element of spiritual self-defense before or during the time he is married with a child or children. Understand that the process of your wife or future wife being like a fruitful vine within your house, and your children being like olive shoots is indicative of their spiritual growth based on your mastery of spiritual self-defense.

Finally, notice how the remaining verses make it clear that you will be blessed as long as you fear the Lord (v. 4), and that he will bless you all the days of your life (v. 5). Finally, verse 5 makes it clear that your mastery of spiritual self-defense will result in your living such a fulfilling life, that you will live to see your children's children. As you continue to train in your mastery of spiritual self-defense, I encourage you to understand that no matter how difficult life can become during this process, as a result of your mastering the spiritual self-defense training instructions from Psalm 128, you and your family will reap wonderful benefits.

Let's get you on the right track with your first spiritual self-defense assignment:

- Talk to a pastor from whom you can seek guidance about what Bible to choose and his or her belief as to how you should conduct your Bible study. Ask him or her to explain the significance of Psalm 128, and how you should effectively apply it to your spiritual self-defense training.

- Begin to read and study the Bible fifteen to thirty minutes a day. Work up to one hour per day. In addition to reading and understanding Psalm 128, I strongly encourage you to read the book of Proverbs, which contains foundational spiritual self-defense tactics that will link to Psalm 128. Also, read Ephesians 6. Study and work to understanding what it means to put on the full armor of God. Also, make sure you understand how to apply this armor to your life.

- Find a Bible-teaching, Bible-believing church. Go to weekly Bible study and church services.

- Memorize and speak additional scripture that applies to what is taking place in your life, and that adds value to the spiritual self-defense training you are undergoing as a result of reading and understanding Psalm 128.

- Right away, apply Bible teaching to your daily Christian walk. Remember to have your guard up *at all times*, being aware that to let it down, would mean to leave a space open for Satan and his demons to go after you. Always being alert and on guard with spiritual self-defense results in the already-defeated enemy having no opening to trick you or have you forget your spiritual "muscle memory."

Chapter 2

The Tongue

*Why What You Say Can Uplift You
or Set You Back*

KING SOLOMON AND ST. James were really on it when they talked about the power of words. Solomon said we are "snared by the words of our mouth" (Prov 6:2). St. James said that "the tongue is a small thing, but what damage it can do" (James 3:5). Dr. Bill Winston is a powerful man of the Lord God who reminds us of the importance of carefully choosing our words. In his book *The Law of Confession*, he explains that we must speak what the Lord God says about us. He states that we must understand that words are more powerful than bombs. If you don't believe that this is case, I want you to do this: think about a thing that someone who is or was close to you said, something so hurtful that it's painful to think about it this very minute. Now, think about some word of encouragement someone you admire said to you that changed your life. In both situations, you remember the words to this very day. You must understand that you, through what you say, have the power to lift others up, or bring them down. The words of others can inspire you to do great things. Words can also kill someone's spirit and literally mentally disable them. Brothers, not only is it important that you speak what the Lord God says about you, you must make sure that you are under the mentorship of other people in the body of Christ; like-minded people who also understand the importance of speaking right.

My earliest recollection of putting this to the test was when I used to collect and read Charles Schultz's *Peanuts* comic strips in paperback form. I had always enjoyed what was a childhood pastime. I couldn't wait to go to the mall with my parents, where I would run to the bookstore with my allowance money to buy the latest paperback. Although I enjoyed the antics of all of the strip characters, I always found myself rooting for Charlie Brown. I wanted to see him win the baseball game, or get to kiss the little red-haired girl he had a crush on. I wanted him to establish meaningful friendships with his peers. Yet, this never happened. As a matter of fact, none of that ever happened. And on of top of that, Charlie Brown always beat himself up verbally, especially after he lost a baseball game, or complained about his lack of friends. I found that the more I followed Charlie Brown's adventures, the more I started to speak like him whenever I found myself on the losing end of a baseball or a kickball game.

Yet, I found that as I became an adolescent, stopped collecting those books, and started to believe my parents' words that I am a winner, and that I could accomplish anything I could put my mind to, that's when things in my life, even as a twelve-year-old boy, began to turn around. I actually began to speak what I wanted, and as long as I believed in what I spoke, and added dedication and determination to the task, I was eventually successful in whatever the endeavor happened to be. The first great remembrance of my success in speaking what I wanted and being successful took place the summer of 1978. Our team was playing in a close game against one of the league rivals. We had played against this team for six years, and had never beaten them. We had played some very competitive games, losing by one or two runs. However, this was the last year of community baseball. The next year we all would be in high school; many of us would be teammates, or would be playing each other in high school competition.

I was the starting pitcher for our team. I remember making up in my mind that on that overcast afternoon, I was going to be the most dominant and most unhittable pitcher they had seen all season. I envisioned and spoke my goal. I remember speaking along these lines: "Nobody's getting a hit against me today. Everything I throw is going to be a strike." I actually remember being mad that day, but in a positive, determined, focused way. I did not throw a no-hitter that day, nor did every pitch I threw wind up being a strike. But I was dominant that day. I don't remember many of the opposing team's players getting a hit, or even reaching first base. They might have scored one run on a throwing error or a sacrifice fly. Still, I was not going to be denied. It seemed contagious. My teammates also gained the same steely resolve. I remember throwing the ball at such a velocity, that our catcher had to wear a pad inside his mitt to keep the ball from stinging the palm of his hand. I just remember strikeout after strikeout. I was in the "zone." I had tunnel vision. I could only see the catcher's mitt. I had blocked out everything else around me. After another strikeout, the players on the opposing team's bench started to walk out onto the field. "What is this?" I thought. "Why are they walking out onto the field?" I said to myself. It was then that I realized that the game was over, and we had won. I shall never forget the success of that day, all because my parents' "training me up in the way that I should go" (Prov 22:6) and telling me about the importance of speaking what I want (Prov 18:21).

Brothers, I want you to understand the power that you have; there really is a miracle in your mouth. You program your mind with your mouth, and not the other way around. If we as Christian men really want to be the best husbands, the best fathers, and the best community leaders we can be, then we first must begin the process of speaking it into existence. It is true that success happens when opportunity and preparedness meet. At the same time, we must speak that we are prepared to successfully take on the task, ready to be proactive in taking advantage of the opportunity, and therefore, speaking success, and being successful.

Brothers, I hope you can see the importance of speaking what you want. Many professional athletes, entertainers, and politicians who are Christian brothers just like you, have talked about the importance of doing this. Former NFL player Deion Sanders, who played on two different Super Bowl champion teams, talks about this important factor. Former Baltimore Ravens linebacker Ray Lewis, also a Super Bowl champion, does the same. I remember, upon meeting Ray Lewis in 2005 at a fitness boot camp sponsored by Empowerment Temple AME Church's men's ministry, how passionate he was about mentoring other men, and working to be the best Christian example he could possibly be. The main thing I remember about Ray Lewis really taking his spiritual growth to another level was how after our pastor, Dr. Jamal H. Bryant, became what I saw as a spiritual father to him, and discipled him in his renewed Christian walk, the world seemed to have seen a change in how he publicly looked to the hills from which come his strength, realizing that all of his strength really comes from his relationship with the Lord (Ps 121:1–2). During the time he spent with us that day, after putting us through a very intense workout (at the time, I was one of two men in their forties, and hadn't had a workout that intense since I played football in the 1980s!), he shared with us Bible-based points about how a real man in the kingdom of the Lord God is supposed to act: a strong man who loves the Lord and treats others the way they want to be treated. At the same time, Ray stated that the same man strives to be like Jesus was when he was on earth, loved humanity, but disciplined them when needed, such as when he dealt with the money-changers who were conducting business transactions in the temple and defiling the Lord God's house (Matt 21:12–13). When I was listening to him, I remember when back in 2000, he was on trial for being an accessory to murder. During the Super Bowl weekend in Atlanta, two of his friends were involved in a brawl, resulting in the stabbing deaths of two men. He was acquitted of the charges. Yet, I and others noticed that after that terrible time in his life, he began to change his associates, choosing to form relationships with people such as Dr. Bryant, who has seemed to be one of his spiritual fathers. The biggest influence regarding his Christian walk that I remember seeing was the 2013 AFC Playoffs; an intense game between the Baltimore Ravens and the Denver Broncos. I remember seeing the Ravens tie the game before the end of regulation time. Afterward, the captains of both teams met the referees in the middle of the field for the explanation of the overtime rules and the coin toss. While the referees were going through the explanation, I remember hearing Ray Lewis continually repeat the phrase "no weapon," saying it over and over again. Right away I knew he was speaking scripture, saying what the Lord God says about him. He was referring to Isaiah 54:17, which states, "No weapon formed against you shall prosper." I knew that Ray was stating that no matter what challenges he is facing at that time, and will ever face, he had learned that the Lord God loves him so much that although Satan's weapons are going to be formed against him, on and off the field, the Lord God was going to make sure that as long as we spoke that none of those weapons formed against him will prosper, that is what would happen. Ray Lewis's speaking this truth about him was profound. Millions of viewers heard him speak this scripture, and millions saw him and the Baltimore Ravens win that overtime playoff game, becoming the AFC Champions. And in his last game as a player, they saw his team, the Baltimore Ravens, win Super Bowl XLVII. The world saw another example of the power of a Christian man speaking what the Lord God says about him through speaking the truth that is in Scripture and showing how it positively works in his life.

They are the first to say that when they were in troubled times, their speaking what the Lord God says about them helped to pull them through, and propel them to true success. Ruben Studdard, 2003 *American Idol* winner, always speaks along these lines, giving all glory and honor to the Lord God, and speaking what the Lord God has spoken about him. Boston Celtics coach Doc Rivers rallied his team around the African word *ubuntu*, which means "I am because we are," and made sure they spoke this during every practice and game. And finally, former president Barack Obama, a Christian African American man, ran a campaign on the words "yes we can," speaking those words into existence by becoming the first African American president of the United States.

So here's your next assignment, regarding your spiritual self-defense training. I only have one task for you, yet it is an important one:

- Open your Bible, and turn to the book of Proverbs. Take a pen or, preferably, a highlighting marker, and underline or highlight every time you see any word that talks about speaking right.

- Afterward, go back and read these scriptures. You will see an important pattern, regarding the importance of making sure you are truly speaking what the Lord God says about you.

Chapter 3

Don't Get It Twisted

When You're Smart, You're Following the Lord God and You're Cool!

My Brothers in Christ, don't get it twisted. Understand that reading, growing as a human being, learning new things, and doing well academically is a good thing. As a matter of fact, it is of the Lord God. It does not mean you're "soft," not cool, or that you're trying to be a "wannabe." You must understand that Satan, your enemy, is the number one manufacturer of "haterade." He works through other people, some of your peers, and some of your so-called friends or your crew, to try to make you feel bad about doing something positive that will improve your life. Don't believe it, brother. Don't purposely mess up in school for fear of what your boys will say. There is a treasure trove of information for success in those books in the classroom and in the library. Reading, for example, will open up a wonderful world for you.

Don't believe it? Okay. For those of you who may be in doubt about this, let's talk about the economic part of it. Most people who are financially successful long-term are people who are readers. There are books out there that, once you read them, they can actually teach you how to be financially secure and successful, for example! Here's a case in point. I once read about two brothers who wanted to learn about winemaking. They walked into a local library and found a book about the process. They really took to heart that book's information. You might recognize their names: Ernest and Julio Gallo. Their wines are world class and world renowned. Their journey to financial success all started due to their acquiring the information through reading.

Starting with my father, every Christian man I know who is and has ever been a mentor to me has always stressed the importance of reading, acquiring knowledge, and getting as much education as possible. I have always been taught that once I sought an area of interest in my life, I should read everything I can get my hands on about it, and seek people who are already successful at it. I should then submit to their leadership and mentorship. Upon receiving that mentor's guidance, I should continually prepare myself for the day that the opportunity would come for me to succeed in the area for which I had prepared. I have followed this formula, and it works. My father, Clyde Stearns, and his brothers, (too many to name, but great role models, too) my uncles on my mother's side of the family, Lt. Col. Hardy Griffin Jr., and the late Dr. Harry Taliaferro, and my godfather, the late Douglas Brown, were all members of the village of strong Christian men whose mentorship is priceless; mentorship that guided me to success as a boy and a man. I don't even want to think of where I would be now without their being a major part of the equation.

In addition, reading inspirational and positive books and listening to speeches by Christian men I admire has also been a part of my circle of mentorship. The sermons of Dr. Bill Winston and the books of Dr. Jawanza Kunjufu have all helped to guide my journey, too. What do all my mentors have in common besides being strong men? They all have always stressed the Lord God-centered advice and have passed it on to me. Their advice emphasized the same point: as long as your endeavor is blessed by the Lord, and is good in his sight, continue to do what you love, and success will come. Work hard, work smart, don't offer up excuses, and learn from others who are in a position you want to be; people who have already achieved notoriety in the field in which you are striving to make a mark. This is the recipe for success.

Now I know brothers, that there are many of you who did not have your father in your life. I understand that many of you have a tremendous amount of pain you have had to deal with because your father did not raise you, even though you are thankful for everything your mother, your grandparents, or a loving guardian has done. I have seen this reality played out in the Washington, DC, area neighborhood where my wife and I used to live, now in South Carolina where I live, and as an associate professor in higher education. I have been on the receiving end of experiencing just what misguided young men are capable of doing. In early November 2004, my wife was robbed at gunpoint right outside our house in Mount Rainier, Maryland, a neighborhood literally down the street from Washington, DC. Four young males were the culprits. She was not harmed, thank the Lord God. In early July 2008, in a case of mistaken identity, my parents' St. Petersburg, Florida, home was riddled with over eighty bullets from an AK-47 assault rifle. My mother was home at the time. Bullets flew by so close to her, that one took off locks of her hair. These people were gunning for our neighbors; young males who were related to a man who was once South Florida's biggest drug kingpin, and were apparently following down the same negative path as their criminal relative. I thank the Lord every day that my wife and mother were not injured in each of those horrible situations. The Baltimore area university campus where I used to be employed would regularly experience a rash of muggings and strong-arm robberies. Nearly all the victims were students, while the culprits were usually described as young males between seventeen and twenty-two years of age.

It is difficult to write about the attacks on my family and students. Yet, I know it's necessary to address the problem in order to correct it and battle it along spiritual lines. I believe that most of these males have not received proper parental guidance in their lives. Many of these young misguided males look to older misguided brothers, the "OGs," or "original gangstas," as role models; the neighborhood drug dealers and gang leaders, who many times are one and the same. The few that did have positive role models, and chose to act out negatively might have had an overburdened grandparent doing the best they could to raise them and do the work of their absent sons or daughters, with little success; I have friends, many of them who are believers who are grandparents of youngsters like these. These grandparents are tired people who should be enjoying their retirement, instead of wondering whether or not their grandson is going to the cemetery or a prison cell. Notice that I call these misguided brothers males, and not men. These guys are not men. *Real* men *don't* do what they do. They do this, because first of all, I don't believe they know what a real man looks like, since many did not have their fathers there to raise and guide them. Many come from well-meaning salt-of-the-earth mothers who are doing their very best to raise their sons and keep them away from the streets. I commend these mothers; the Lord God knows I do. Still, some come from homes where in some cases, even the mother has not done her job as a parent. The bottom line is that whether they're mother-of-the-year types, or whether that's not the case, they cannot teach them to be men. Only a Lord God-centered man, a real man, can guide these young males in the ultimate right direction that leads to understanding and applying spiritual self-defense.

This is the "for real for real": Satan is trying to destroy young males. He is trying to do this through lack of mentorship and manhood training due to absentee fathers and not enough positive men who are role models in the community. Christian men in the community must join forces to turn the tide. I have been blessed that one of my mentors, a strong, Lord God-fearing man, encouraged me to pray every day for those responsible for the attacks on my wife and mother. It has helped me to grow as a Christian, knowing that forgiveness of others, too, is what the Lord commands.

For example, if I *really* wanted to exact revenge on many former enemies, I could do so, with no problem. With online white pages and various search engines online, it is now easier than ever to find just about anyone. Yet, I have won that spiritual battle by exercising the spiritual self-defense lesson taught by the late Dale

Carnegie in his book *How to Stop Worrying and Start Living*. In one of his chapters he states that when you try to exact revenge on your enemies, you hurt yourself more than you hurt them. He goes on to explain that mere health problems such as heart disease and ulcers, as well as hypertension can be a result of resentment. I was dumbstruck when I read a passage about a restaurant owner who became so angry at an employee he chased him around the restaurant and fell dead from a heart attack! I learned a valuable lesson about forgiveness. We should do it not only because the Lord commands it; we should do it because the Lord wants us to live victoriously, which includes being in good health! I am not going to have resentment to the point that it puts me in an early grave, and neither should you!

To further emphasize this point, several years ago, during my Baltimore area teaching days I encountered a situation where one of my students, a young man, came to me with a problem. He had just come back from his home in New Jersey. He left to deal with a family emergency. A young misguided male in his neighborhood had shot his younger sister with a BB gun. Although his sister was going to successfully heal from minor injuries, he shared with me that he wanted to get back at the one responsible. I shared with him the situation I had gone through, and how I struggled with similar feelings. I assured him that the Lord God would deal with those responsible; it's his call, not ours (Romans 10:19). He thanked me for my words, and chose to leave it in the Lord's hands. I did not know his walk; whether he was a Christian or not. Yet, I did know he believed in the Lord God. This encounter showed me how the Lord uses Christian men's testimonies and their experiences to minister to other Christian brothers who are going through similar situations. I thank the Lord that he spoke to that young student of mine. Not only did he pass my classes, he is also an up-and-coming recording artist and producer! The Lord has placed it on my heart that he will continue to be around to be a blessing to others.

Brothers, the Bible tells us to "testify to what we have seen" (John 3:11). I have seen Christian brothers become successful and remain successful because they allowed themselves to be mentored by other Christian brothers who are in a position spiritually where they want to be. Once you've got it together spiritually, everything else falls into place. Are things going to just stop being difficult? No. You will still have your ups and downs; yet now, you'll know how to deal with things because you'll be doing it the Lord God's way, and not your way. I cannot stress this enough, brothers. Hang around people in the body of Christ who've got your back. Let's seek to encourage and mentor those Christian brothers, and those who we want to bring to Christ. The Bible tells us that "as iron sharpens iron, so one man sharpens another" (Prov 27:17).

Brothers, we cannot let the enemy consume us. Remember, Satan "goes about like a roaring lion, seeking whom he can devour" (1 Pet 5:8). Christian men of all ages must be the warriors of the Lord God in our communities, allowing him to work through us and turn the tide of violence, despair, underachievement, addiction, and abandonment that too many brothers are enduring. It's time for us to rely on the omnipotent, omnipresent, and omniscient Lord God that we serve to help us to put a beatdown on an already-defeated devil. Remember, the Bible says that we are already victorious. One of his names is Jehovah Nisei, our God of victory; a name that Moses used to celebrate his victory, literally meaning "the Lord is my banner" (Exod 17:15). Moses even built an altar with this name to always commemorate his witnessing the Lord's granting him, despite challenges and setbacks, victorious living! The Lord God wants every Christian man to be a leader in our community; one who is successful because he teaches other Christian brothers to be leaders. That's the true Lord God-centered nature of the real Christian man. Let's take our rightful place as mentors and builders of our community.

Do you want to know how you can do this? You must continue to work on your spiritual self-defense, of course! Here is your next assignment, designed to get you to where your skills need to be:

- Pray for *every one of your enemies* for thirty days. Even if you're not feeling like doing this, do it. Don't trust me on this;

trust the Lord God. You must let go of the spirit of vengeance, and replace it with a spirit of love and forgiveness. This is how you begin to learn one of your greatest self-defense techniques; replacing what Satan meant for evil, with what the Lord God means for good (Gen 50:15–21)!

- Don't let the day go by without telling *at least one person you know in some way* that you appreciate them. It does not matter whether that person is a Christian, whether you know him that well, or if you don't know him at all. It could be the custodian at your job, the usher at your church, the convenient store employee, or a coworker. Throughout the day, too many people hear enough negative; let's demonstrate the Lord God's love and give each other some positive reinforcement.

- Volunteer to work on a Lord God-centered project *at least once a month* with other Christian brothers. The men's ministry at your church may be conducting a mentoring session with at-risk young people, for example. The church may be sponsoring an SAT preparation seminar, or college preparatory tutoring. If you're in need of mentoring, seek Christian men in your community who run Christ-centered programs in which you can grow in your knowledge and application of spiritual self-defense.

- Call up or visit someone in your family. Tell them you love them, and that you are praying for them. Do it *today*.

Chapter 4

Training Up

You Must Raise Your Children Right, No Matter What

BROTHERS, WE IN THE body of Christ must be a part of setting things straight; raising the children we bring into the world is a primary example of this. The Bible tells us to "train up a child in the way that they should go, so when they become old, they will not depart from this" (Prov 22:6). The Bible also says, "Fathers, do no exasperate your children. Instead, bring them up in the training and instruction of the Lord" (Eph 6:4). We are dealing with many young adults who were exasperated children; exasperated because their fathers were barely in their lives or not at all. Exasperated children carry that pain way beyond their childhood years; many become exasperated adults. I once saw a former pastor at a church shed tears, while in the pulpit, he recalled the pain of his father not being there for him. Thankfully, his story was one of triumph and victory, for he found the true foundation in his Heavenly Father, who directed him to mentorship from strong Christian men throughout his life. Many men don't have that structure, yet they still can seek and receive it. We must raise our children to be the best Christians they can be. As I mentioned previously, I know that there are many of you who are fathers who did not have your own

father in your life. I understand that those of you who are dealing
with this may not know what to do. If this is you, I encourage you
to seek the mentorship of a Christian brother who is married, or
single and is preferably living with or nearby his children, who is a
good father who's always there for his offspring. If his children are
in another state with the mother, and there is strong evidence that
he is seeing them frequently, then that is acceptable, too. As long
as others in the body of Christ also look to the brother for advice
and guidance, that is a good sign that perhaps you should, too. Let
the Holy Spirit guide you, here. If you have a good feeling about
the brother's Christian walk, and if he's willing to give you advice
on how to successfully raise your child, then that may be the Holy
Spirit letting you know that this is a good brother to receive spiritual advice and guidance. This brother could be a pastor, a school
principal, a maintenance worker in the neighborhood, or a police
officer. It does not matter what he does, as long as he is a good
Christian example in the community who is successfully raising
his children and being an active part of their life. Jesus told us in
the Bible that "a tree is known by its fruit" (Matt 7:16–20). That
brother, who even may be a Christian, may be someone you admire. At the same time, that brother may be doing some things that
he needs to go to the Lord for some "pruning." Bruce Wilkinson, in
his book *Secrets of the Vine* reminds us that just like the grapevine
that needs to be pruned in order to produce more fruit, we in the
body of Christ need constant pruning, or cutting away of things in
our life that are not the Lord God's will. You may know a Christian
brother who is making strides in some areas of his life. Yet he is
not an active part of his child's life. Or he may not be disciplining
his children as the Bible instructs. Don't follow his example. At
the same time, don't judge him either. Love on him, pray for him,
and ask the Lord to keep on pruning the unproductive vines in his
life. Continue to seek and find a brother who is an example of raising his children according to Christian principles. Observe how
his children act around you and others; this is a good indicator.
Brothers, just exercise your spirit of discernment. Ask the Lord
to lead you to Christian brothers who are the right example you

should follow. Remember there are Christian brothers whose walk is one of growth and learned lessons, and those who are not "walking the walk"; make sure you choose the former.

For example, my wife and I do not have children. If the Lord sees fit for us to be parents, that process will happen in his time. We know that if it does happen, the Lord God has already blessed me with being around strong Christian fathers who will offer me godly, Bible-based advice regarding child-rearing. My own biological father, a good, God-fearing man, will be, right after my Heavenly Father, the second father of whom I seek advice and guidance. Take my word for it; even with two loving Christian parents (who have been married for fifty-eight years!) loving me and training me up, I was *still* a handful as a child. The Lord God working through my parents got me through to adulthood in solid shape, thank the Lord God. I probably would have been dead or in prison had it not been for my parents' love and guidance. And although my mother always went the extra mile for me, and loved me unconditionally, and is the greatest mother a child could ever have, only my father could have taught me to be a man. I am eternally grateful to both of my parents. Yet, Dad taught me the for real for real, when it comes to the Lord God working through him to transition me from boyhood to manhood. Sometimes those lessons were taught with words; sometime the lesson was learned by the application of a belt onto my behind (I deserved every one of those whippings, too!). Nevertheless, it was all done in love. There's something else I want to share as well. If you are living with the mother of your child, and if you love that woman, I am not judging you, or your situation, but I want your family to receive the full benefit of the Lord God's blessings. If you don't love her, and you still want to make sure that your child, the mother of your child, and you receive all of the blessings that the Lord God the Father, the Lord God the Son, and the Lord God the Holy Spirit have for you, I encourage you to move out of that house and live nearby. You may not even want to hear that, but it's for your own good, and for the good of your family. The fact of the matter is that it's biblical. The Bible tells us that "the marriage bed must be left pure" (Heb 13:4).

If you want your son or daughter to grow up to live by Christian principles, the sanctity of marriage, and being that good example of not living in sin has to be in the mix, too. That child is not going to know what a good marriage is, or what a good marriage looks like if they don't see one. I encourage you to seek every good thing that the Lord God has for your child, and you want to train up him or her with the understanding that the Lord God wants the very best for them.

Again, I want to make it perfectly clear that I am not judging those of you who are working through these types of situations. I have experienced similar ones. When I was in my early twenties I once found out after the fact from a former girlfriend that I had gotten her pregnant, and she miscarried. It happened while we were undergraduate students. She was in her last year in school, and I had another year to go. She never told me until a few years later when I was in graduate school in the Washington, DC, area, and she was immersed in her career as a successful journalist in Columbus, Ohio. When I asked her why she never told me, she said that since she miscarried after a short time, she never felt the need at the time to do so. I said to her that I still would have wanted to have known about it. The Lord God knows that if she had had that child, I would have moved to Columbus, Ohio, to make sure I was there to do my part, regarding raising that child. Even though I later realized that I was not in love with her, I would have fallen in love with the act of co-parenting; either marrying her out of a sense of doing what needed to be done, if the Lord God willed it, or definitely living nearby and always being in my child's life. I would have done that because I was taught by other Christian men, that this is the right thing to do. There were men who either were divorced from their children's mother, or in some cases, didn't marry their child's mother at all. However, they loved their child or children, and they exemplified that love by making sure they were nearby to do their part in raising and properly training them up.

I can also speak about the whole "shacking' up" thing. On two occasions, for a short period of time, I lived in sin, with two women from different times in my life. Regardless of the circumstances, as a Christian, I knew that it was wrong. As a matter of fact, I did not experience a continuance of more of the Lord God's blessings in my life until I stopped doing it. And I can tell you with no degree of uncertainty and hesitation that when I lived with these women, I was no choirboy. I was a back-sliding dude who was robbing himself of blessings. Once I "righted the ship," stopped this behavior, and got back on track, the Lord God saw fit to bless me with many other things that were good in his sight.

In addition, I also want to refer to what the Bible says about men who don't want to be married. The Apostle Paul, who never married, made it clear that it is acceptable for a man to stay single. At the same time, he made it clear that even a single man must strive to be the proper example in the Lord God's kingdom:

> I wish that all of you were as I am. But each of you has your own gift from the Lord God; one has this gift, another has that. Now to the unmarried and the widows I say: It is good for them to stay unmarried, as I do. But if they cannot control themselves, they should marry, for it is better to marry than to burn with passion. (1 Cor 7:7–9)

I knew that I was the kind of guy who wanted to do the Lord God's will, but would take a female to bed out of wedlock if the opportunity arose. So I prayed to the Lord, show me who my wife was to be so that I would find her, love her, honor her, cherish her, and of course, marry her. When the Lord created the situation in which he introduced me through his divine circumstances to my lovely wife, Karen, I was relieved. I had had it with the struggle of being a single Christian man. I knew that I didn't have the Apostle Paul's discipline, so I knew that once I married Karen, the eros love, that erotic love, along with that heartfelt cherishing agape love was there, and would always be there. That was 2002. We got married in holy matrimony on January 3, 2004. Over fifteen years later, I am a happily married, monogamous man; one who is so glad that he stopped leaning onto his own understanding, and took the time to seek the Lord God for finding his soul mate!

When it comes to marriage, I thank the Lord God that it is the most rewarding challenge that I'll ever love. It takes work, and I am thankful that the Lord has given my wife, Karen, and me the Bible, the greatest instruction book for spiritual self-defense. We both work together, and we are committed for life to studying and learning its principles. We realize that every day is not going to be a perfect day, but we always look to the Lord God the Father, the Lord God the Son, and the Lord God the Holy Spirit for guidance. When we have disagreements, we make sure that we are not nasty toward one another. Sometimes, in the midst of a disagreement, the Holy Spirit will either tell us to walk away and talk about the disagreement later, once we've taken the time to think about the spiritually correct way to resolve the disagreement; or sometimes the argument may begin to go in such a negative direction that we will verbally declare a time out, because we realize that Satan, our enemy, is trying to stir up dissention and unhealthy anger in our marriage. Upon that realization, too, we'll either discuss the matter later in a civil way, or we'll pause, verbally rebuke Satan in the name of Jesus, and then, we'll continue to work to resolve the disagreement, working to reach a civil solution. Another key method of spiritual self-defense we practice is the act of never going to bed angry. Scripture backs up this important point, too. The Bible says, "In your anger, do not sin. Do not let the sun go down while you're still angry" (Eph 4:26). This spiritual self-defense technique is another crucial one, because Satan will take your anger, which you take to bed, and have you hang onto it the next morning, and in many cases, days, weeks, or years. This matter that one can take to bed while they are angry, if not dealt with, can turn into a resentment; one that could be long term, and detrimental to the marriage. Therefore, here's another spiritual self-defense technique you must master.

At the same time, I want you men who are not married to practice this, too. If you are single, make sure you, in your singleness, also resolve that you are not going to go to bed angry. Whatever is angering you, make sure you read what the Bible says as to how you should successfully deal with the situation so that you are not angry when it's bedtime. Look in the Bible for the solution to ridding yourself of anger. Most Bibles have a concordance in the back. Look for the word *anger*, and then read what the Bible says as to how a Christian deals with it. In addition to doing that, I've used the book *Touch Points for Men*, which has an index with many biblical topics. Once you find your topic, the index lets you know what page to turn to, where you will see your topic, the related scripture, and written advice, as well.

What does the previous information have to do with your relationship to your children? It is a big deal, because at times, it can be easy for a Christian man who's a single parent, who is doing the right thing, to be tempted to engage in baby-mama drama. Whatever you do, don't allow your child to see you and the mother of your child arguing. You must remember that children's minds are like sponges; they suck up every bit of information that is presented within their presence. They are going to emulate a lot of what they see in their parents' behavior. If the behavior is negative, they could possibly repeat either being a perpetrator or victim of that negative behavior. For example, I know women who saw their fathers disrespect their mothers by horribly negative actions such as domestic violence, and adultery. What do you think happened when these women grew up? They married, and then divorced men who domestically abused them and/or cheated on them with other women, or sometimes stayed in that unhealthy relationship. Now that is an extreme example. Yet, even if your child sees you and their mother arguing, then that sends the message that a normal interaction between parents is supposed to go down that way, and that's a lie out of the pit of Hell. The fact of the matter is that Christian couples have disagreements just like other couples. At the same time, it is the responsibility of a Christian married couple especially to show the right example by following what the Bible says about resolving any couples-related conflict.

Again, although disagreements will surface, and you and your mate must handle them by the instruction of the Bible, always remember, I must emphasize again, that under no circumstances should you argue, fuss, and fight with the mother of your child in front of the child. When you feel tempted to argue, remember that the Bible says that "a gentle answer turns away wrath, but a harsh word stirs up anger" (Prov 15:1). Let your child see you taking the steps of practicing spiritual self-defense with your words. When you practice this, you are engaging in another action that is indicative of doing everything you are supposed to do to love that child, be there for that child, and being civil and cordial with the mother, whether she returns it or not. I know good, married Christian brothers who have children from previous relationships. They love, nurture, and are fully present in those children's lives. They know that it's not easy, but they also know that it's the toughest job they'll ever love. No matter what, you must raise the children you bring into the world. The Bible requires all parents to "start children off the way that they should go, and even when they are old, they won't turn from it" (Prov 22:6). Also, as stated previously, the Bible reminds men who are fathers "not to exasperate your children; instead, bring them up in the training and instruction of the Lord" (Eph 6:4). As I mentioned previously, I can truthfully testify that as an educator even in the university classroom, I come across many students who were exasperated children because hypothetically, I believe that their parents did not bring them up in the training and instruction of the Lord, and now these same individuals are exasperated adults who at times will bring their emotional strongholds on campus.

Brothers, you must understand that bringing children into the world and not raising them is against what the Lord God commands. We must break the vicious cycle of the generational curses of absentee fatherhood in our communities. If Christian men don't stand up and be an example here, who will? Brothers, even if you did not see good husbands and fathers in your family, look for it somewhere, and follow that example! Please! The survival of our community depends on our stopping this generational curse! Satan wants to break up our families, leaving children without the full nurturing and guidance they need and deserve! He wants there to be as many broken homes and broken lives in our community as possible. The Lord God of our salvation wants strong loving families in our community, with loving parents successfully raising their children so that they can be beneficial to the community. Let's remain on the Lord's side, and strengthen our families through the proper nurturing of our children! And by the way: I don't apologize for repeating scriptural references in this book. You need repetition and practice to strengthen your spiritual self-defense.

Now it's time for the next spiritual self-defense lesson for all you fathers. Here it is:

- Seek fatherhood instructional classes in your church, or in the community; classes in which positive Christian fathers can instruct you on how to be the best Christian father you can be.

- Volunteer your time with one of the youth ministries of your church, so you can participate in and benefit from activities that show other Christian men nurturing either their own children, or children whose fathers are not in their lives.

- Seek membership in Christian organizations where you will encounter Christian men who are successfully raising and nurturing their children.

Chapter 5

The Gentle Answer Means
That You Are Strong

*Tapping into the Holy Spirit So You Can
Poison Satan's "Haterade"*

THE BIBLE VERSE THAT I mentioned previously about the gentle answer turning away wrath is one that I have used with great success, and have seen other Christian brothers do likewise. I have been in similar situations where, on the job, I have had to deal with rude, misguided males wanting to commence various altercations with me; ones that have come dangerously close to placing me in a possible self-defense situation. I must say that when it comes to this, my Christian walk of the past has still not been one where I have always fully turned the other cheek. I am more than capable of defending myself, and I am a great believer in self-preservation and self-defense. However, one must use common sense. Whether it is the workplace, or other environments, one does not want to place their livelihood in jeopardy and go to jail or face a civil suit, and one does not know who is and who is not armed. Remember brothers; there is no longer such a thing as a fair fight anymore, unless you are a boxer, kick boxer, or a mixed martial artist. Again, you don't want to do anything to lose your job, nor do you want to place yourself in a situation that might get you stabbed or shot. There are too many unsaved people out there, whose self-esteem is so low, who consciously or subconsciously can't wait to get sent away to prison on a murder charge. Let's use wisdom and common sense, be firm and assertive in our speech and love and pray for our enemies, and live to fight the good fight of faith another day!

I wished I would have not seen the recent results that demonstrate the opposite of this situation. When my wife and I still lived in the Washington, DC, area, when watching the news, the television stations would cover happenings in suburban Maryland and northern Virginia, as well as the District. The other day, I saw a news report of a shoot-out at a northern Virginia bus terminal. The shoot-out allegedly took place between two bus drivers who at one time were the best of friends. The result was that one of the men shot and killed the other, then turned himself in to the authorities. A few months earlier, a similar situation happened between two area firefighters. They got into an argument during a card game at a private residence. One shot the other to death, and was recently arrested.

Seeing these two situations reminds me of the fact that homicide, in the form of fratricide, male-on-male homicide, is the number one killer of many males in this country. I believe that young and older men in the kingdom of the Lord God, by calling on and having the Father, Son, and Holy Spirit working through them can stop this occurrence. Spiritual self-defense is much stronger than physical self-defense. The only reason I have not served time for disorderly conduct for fighting other men in the streets or elsewhere in the past has everything to do with my spiritual self-defense. As I said before, I'm still working on the turn-the-other-cheek part of my Christian walk. If someone corners me, and does not give me the option to leave the situation, then physically accosts me, and if I believe they're not armed, I'm going to defend myself to the best of my ability. That's common sense. As I mentioned before, I'm still a work in progress regarding Jesus' instructions to turn the other cheek (Matt 5:38–40). Yet I always do my best to talk my way out of a situation by using the soft answer to turn away wrath. When you do this, it does not mean you're "soft" or a "wimp." If you handle situations like that the world's way, chances are you could wind up like that bus driver and that firefighter who are likely to spend several years behind bars due to a serious lapse in judgment.

Yet, we as men in the body of Christ can give the devil a nervous breakdown by ignoring his "haterade" tactics. He can't stand to see men in unity, especially Christian men. As a matter of fact, there is scripture that backs up this wonderful happening that give the enemy such grief. The scripture says, "How good and pleasant it is when God's people live together in unity!" (Ps 133:1). Although this is from the New International Version of the Bible, as is all scripture in this book, there are other translations that interpreted as men coming together in unity. When we as Christian men come together in unity, memorize self-defense scripture, and apply it to our lives, not only will it continue to give Satan a nervous breakdown; it will result in our being the example that other Christian men, especially those who are struggling, and feeling as though they're not winning spiritual warfare, will need to see. It will cause those who attempt to push our buttons to realize that, through spiritual self-defense, we have something that they may want. If these same "button-pushers" are not Christians, they, upon seeing what we have, may want to know what they must do to be saved, and have the kind of relationship that we have with God the Father, God the Son, and God the Holy Spirit. Why? Because they could have Satan lying to them since they don't have enough power to do anything to someone who has the power of the Lord God on their side. They may be able to form some kind of weapon toward we, who are God's people, but the Bible makes it very clear that "no weapon forged against you will prevail" (Isa 54:17). There have been times where I have stated the facts about a situation that have also resulted in the application of this scripture-as-spiritual-self-defense tactic that states, "Then you will know the truth, and the truth shall set you free" (John 8:32). The Lord God's word and the Lord God's truth in any situation, you must "submit yourselves, then, to the Lord God" and "resist the devil and he will flee from you" (James 4:7). You're not a pushover; you're powerful. You're not "soft" or "wimpy"; you're strong, and a warrior on the front lines of the battlefield for the Lord, strong in his almighty, infinite power. We are engaged in spiritual warfare. Listen to the right voice, the voice of the Lord God, and you will be just fine. It is not easy at times, but it's the right thing to do. The weapons are going to be formed against you, but you are learning just what to do when this happens, knowing that you will be victorious in the Lord over that non-prevailing weapon.

So we now go to the next spiritual self-defense practice tactic. Here's what I want you to do now:

- Look up and memorize any scripture in the Bible you can actually speak, when faced with a confrontational situation that you want to handle the right way.

- Get into the habit of prefacing your words with "surely" and then "nevertheless." For example, you can say to a confrontational person, "Surely, you don't want us to be arrested for disorderly conduct, do you?" After their answer you can say, "Well nevertheless, I'm squashing this, man. I'm not beefing with you. I am not going to go there with you; I'm walking away from this confrontation. I don't want to go to jail." Speak along these lines in a situation like this, or apply it to the necessary situation.

- Make sure you are prayed up before leaving your place. Ask the Lord to protect you, guide you, and lead you to do and say the right thing. Make sure you thank the Lord God for his armor and his Son Jesus' blood that are on you and protect you. Also, thank the Holy Spirit for being the Comforter that guides you and leads you when it comes to day-to-day and moment-by-moment decisions.

Chapter 6

Putting Away Childish Things

*Now Is The Time to Put an End
to the Lust Problem*

I WANT TO TELL you a story about a man named Solomon; a man of the Lord God who became the biggest "playa" in the world. This man was a wealthy Hebrew king who the Lord God loved and blessed with land, wealth and power beyond a man's wildest dreams. From his yearly gold revenues alone, which was twenty-five tons per year (1 Kgs 10:14) he had a net worth that today would exceed fifteen billion dollars per year. He had so much wealth and power, that probably no man of his time had as much sex with beautiful women from all over the known world. Because of this power, he had access to so many beautiful women, that he would've put the most accomplished modern-day ladies' man to shame. Yet here's the problem. King Solomon used his wealth, power, and influences to allow him access to all of this sex with these women all over the world, resulting in the attention from these women and the sex to negatively affect his relationship with the Lord God. How do I know this? The Bible tells me so. Here is the scripture:

> King Solomon, however, loved many foreign women besides Pharaoh's daughter—Moabites, Ammonites,

> Edomites, Sidonians and Hittites. They were from na-
> tions about which the Lord had told the Israelites, "You
> must not intermarry with them, because they will surely
> turn your hearts after their the Lord Gods." Nevertheless,
> Solomon held fast to them in love. He had seven hundred
> wives of royal birth and three hundred concubines, and
> his wives led him astray. As Solomon grew old, his wives
> turned his heart after other gods, and his heart was not
> fully devoted to the Lord his God, as the heart of David
> his father had been. (1 Kgs 11:1–4)

I want to take this time to really concentrate on the sex part, especially the sex with the concubines. But first, I quickly want to
mention that although he was married to seven hundred of these
women, he was unequally yoked with most of them. He married
women who did not share his love for and belief in the Lord God
of Israel; the Lord God of his and our understanding. I address this
matter further in the chapter that deals specifically with marriage.
Now, getting back to the concubines, here is what compounded
Solomon's problem; his ability to have sex outside of marriage with
these women, with as many as he wanted, either one at a time or
multiple women at the same time, resulted in his concentrating on
having all this sex and not concentrating on what the Lord God
wanted him to do to advance his kingdom. King Solomon allowed
all of this access to sex, especially the concubine, "no strings at-
tached" sex, to divert a significant amount of his time to this, and
little or no significant time to the Lord God's plan for his life, and
the work that the Lord God wanted him to do to advance his work
throughout all of the known world. The same chapter tells us that
the Lord God, in his anger at and disappointment in Solomon, not
only raised up adversaries against Solomon; he told him that after
his death, his kingdom would go to one of his subordinates and
not his son (1 Kgs 11:11–13).

The problem with the lust of the flesh is that it is a selfish
act. Recently, as I was looking up information about it in the book
Touch Points for Men, I came upon a statement that to me summed
up this problem:

> When lust is allowed to take up residence in our minds, it
> tends to consume our thoughts and push the light of the
> Lord God aside. Solomon's lust led not only to promiscu-
> ity but to his turning away from the Lord God. Lust takes
> what it wants, regardless of the other's needs or desires.
> Lust is impatient and rude.[1]

Lust, is part of a larger problem; sin as a generational curse. It is a
generational curse because it is a family pattern. If you are sleeping
around, there have been others in your family who have done and
are probably still doing the same thing, if they're still alive. Brothers, I have been around long enough to know, by my own past
selfishness, and by witnessing the selfishness of others, that lust
really is about an individual wanting what he or she wants, and not
caring about how it affects the other person. Dr. Jawanza Kunjufu
states that when males are young boys, they play with toys such as
video games and other toys, yet when too many of them become
adults, they play with women.[2] Too many adult males, most of
them who are not men, selfishly play with women's emotions, just
to get them into bed, knowing that no long-term relationship, and
definitely not marriage, is not going to come out of it. The problem
is that this is selfish, childish behavior, and should have been done
away with when a male becomes an adult; something that the Bible
makes crystal clear (1 Cor 13:11). We must be reminded that this
kind of behavior is not of the Lord God. Lust is lust; whether it is
premarital sex between a male and a female, two females, or two
males, it is not of the Lord God.

Brothers, let's be real. No matter what the circumstances,
when you are having sex without being married you are playing
a dangerous game on so many levels. I realize we live in a world
that, by its standards, the mind-set is still "if it feels good, do it."
And that is *still* a lie from the pit of Hell. I am not here to judge
anyone; only the Lord God is the judge. I am here to say that if we
men in the body of Christ do not take a stand and live right, and
be the right example for other Christian men and boys, we may

1. Beers, *Touch Points for Men*, 162–63.
2. See Kunjufu, *Developing Positive Self-Images*, 23.

not get chance after chance to get it right! We may die within the next second, minute, hour, or day! Tomorrow is not promised! We don't want to die without getting it right. We especially don't want to be caught slipping when Jesus comes back! Therefore, if you really don't want to practice spiritual self-defense when it comes to this matter as well, then don't say you're a Christian, because you are being hypocritical and disobedient. It is true that the Bible says that "all have sinned, and fall short of the glory of the Lord God (Rom 3:23). At the same time, we cannot justify the sin of lust by using excuses such as "yes we are 'doing it' but we're getting married someday anyway," or "I can't help it, because I was born this way." You may think you were born with certain tendencies, but you must get that out of your mind, because if you are a true Christian, you are born again (John 3:1–21)! I learned that important lesson from my former pastor, Dr. Jamal H. Bryant. We have to stop making excuses, and "man up" and be the Christians that the Lord says we should be!

I know there is much temptation out there, regarding the pressure to have sex before marriage. No matter how much we try to do the right thing, the media, our peers, and even close family members can pressure us about whether or not we are doing this, and some of these people claimed to be saved, too! I am the first to admit this weakness. Before my wife and I met and got married, I had had sex with close to two dozen women. I was not practicing abstinence, nor was I a "playa." I had been saved since I was eleven years old. I even rededicated my life to the Lord at seventeen. Yet, from the time I had lost my virginity at twenty years old, to a few months before with a woman I found to be attractive. The only exception was in college, when I actually chose not to sleep with women who wanted relationships, when all I wanted was the sex. In some of those cases, I walked away without hurting the woman, but in other cases I chose to have as much sex as possible, not caring much about the feelings of the female who wanted a relationship that would inevitably lead to marriage; something I refused to do in my younger years. I was what you would call a "sexual camel." You know how a camel loads up on water before it goes on a long trek without it in the desert? Well, I was like that. I would load up on as much sex as one woman would let me have. While she thought it would be her ticket to getting me to the altar, my mind-set was to get as much sex as possible from the woman until she caught onto my scheme. This was the kind of person I was in my early twenties to early thirties; something I am not proud of. As a matter of fact, not only did I know it was wrong; I would ask the Lord for forgiveness afterward, all the time, knowing that once the opportunity presented itself again, I would go right back to my "camel" ways. At the same time, there was a few times where this bad behavior resulted in a "turnabout is fair play" situation. On more than one occasion, I ran into a situation in which I would meet a woman I really thought could've been "the one" hoping that she saw me as "Mr. Right." It would turn out that she saw me as "Mr. Right Now," later "kicking me to the curb" and ending what I thought was a meaningful relationship.

So I know how difficult it is, brothers. Once I entered my early to mid-thirties, I was ready to settle down. I knew as I had stated previously that the Apostle Paul said in the New Testament that if we cannot control ourselves, we should marry, for it is better to marry than to burn with passion (1 Cor 7:9). I even leaned unto my own understanding, and proposed to a woman with whom I was in a long-distance relationship. I did not go through with the marriage, because I came to realize it was not a relationship that the Lord God had put together. Even after that situation, I slowed down but did not stop the premarital sex part. There were even times that when I became lonely enough, I would actually go to what is known as AMPs: Asian massage parlors. I found them on the internet, and when I could afford to go to them, I would, every now and then. Many offer more than massages, if you know what I mean. Again, even though using protection in the form of condoms is mandatory in those places, and the majority of the women were stunning, I knew it was not only wrong morally, but illegal as well. I later found out from a newspaper story that many of those women were victims of human trafficking; they received the chance to come to America, the land of opportunity to make a better life for them, but had to pay off their "immigration debt" to the one who financed their trip by working in these undercover brothels.

In the midst of my selfishness, the Lord God saw fit to have mercy on me. Although the AMP's required condom use and had them on the premises, when it came to past encounters outside of these establishments, even in the age of AIDS, genital herpes, and other STDs, there were times I had unprotected sex with females. Only by the Lord God's grace and mercy did I not receive an STD.

Again, as I mentioned before, I am ashamed of myself for falling, and backsliding all over the place. I have no excuse; I should have waited to have sex when I got married, even though that did not happen until I turned thirty-nine. Brothers, the most important thing I can say to you is this: don't believe the hype. That whole premarital sex thing is not as big a thing as your peers, the TV set, the movie screen, the internet, and the popular media try to make it out to be. The best sex in the world is the sex that is between you and the woman the Lord God picked for you, in a state of holy matrimony. The last several years of relationships with women before I met my wife was, overall, unfulfilling sexually. It was this way because I knew the Lord God wasn't anywhere in those situations. He was waiting for me to get out of those inappropriate sexual relationships and wait on him so that he, once he found me worthy, would bless me with a Christian wife who has my back. That's exactly what happened. When the Lord saw that I had matured spiritually, and had really made a sincere effort to get right with him, *that's* when he blessed me with my awesome wife, Karen. I am now a happily married man; I love and simply adore my awesome wife whom the Lord God blessed me with for these past fifteen-plus years! I constantly tell her how much I love her, and how she is my gift from the Lord God!

Brothers, please heed my warning. Far too many Christian men are allowing themselves to go down the wrong path, when it comes to the lust problem. Premarital sex is not of the Lord God. I am not judging those of you who are struggling with this. We must learn spiritual self-defense in order to overcome these feelings and actions. The Apostle Paul made it clear that we in the body of Christ have only two choices when it comes to sex; either sex with your wife, or abstinence (1 Cor 7:1–5). The Lord God loves us, and he wants us to make the right choices. Jesus spent a considerable amount of time ministering along these lines, making sure that he emphasized that it is not about judging people (Matt 7:1–6). He told the judgmental Pharisees that it is the sick that are in need of a doctor (Matt 9:12). Our first line of spiritual self-defense is to pray frequently, and ask the Lord to deliver us from *all* forms of lust. Again, I must make it crystal clear that I am not judging a single person. I am referring to what our greatest spiritual self-defense weapon, the Sword of the Spirit, which is the Word of God, says to all men in God's kingdom.

Many of you may see this as unrealistic. It is not. Paul was a great example of this. He never married, and for the rest of his life, was, by all accounts, a man who practiced what he preached. Dr. Charlene Monk once preached that the thorn Paul had in his side might have been something he was struggling with spiritually, and not a physical ailment.[3] Whether this was or was not the case, it is clear that by his walk, when Paul gave his life to the Lord, he became equipped to overcome the spiritual thorn in his side. Gospel recording artist and pastor Donnie McClurkin struggled with and overcame the personal fallout stemming from being raped and sexually abused by men when he was a child. When rock-and-roll legend Little Richard accepted Jesus Christ as his personal Lord and Savior, he overcame former struggles, and gave his live to Jesus. In Tye Tribbett's popular song "I Got the Victory," as his group Greater Anointing sings, "Whatever it is, you've got to comeooooooooooouuuuuuutttt," he shouts out, among other important pleas related to coming out of all forms of sin, including the lust of the flesh. Remember brothers: you are not a slave to sin of any kind. Brother Tribbett and Greater Anointing remind us that whatever sin we are struggling with, we have got to come out of

---

3. From a sermon titled "Monkey on My Back," by Dr. Charlene Monk, pastor, New Horizons Christian Faith Church, Mount Rainier, Maryland, http://newhorizoncfc.org/.

it *now*. My brother and his group knows that we have the victory over sin, and we just have to exercise the power that is in the name of Jesus, and call on our Lord and savior to deliver us from all the sinful junk that's out there in the world.

Lust is a spiritual thorn. I struggled with this all the way up until several months before my marriage. I wanted to make love to my future wife all the time before we got married. It wasn't until my future brother-in-law and sister-in-law called my fiancée and me out on this. About six months before my wife and I got married, she, I, and my future in-laws decided to spend Memorial Day weekend in a rented condo in the Poconos. After hearing certain sounds coming from our room the night before, my future brother- and sister-in-law decided to later sit us down and remind us of the importance of waiting to have sex when we got married. They had a right to talk to us. The Bible says that the Lord God disciplines us in love, so that means that when he sees fit to do so, he can work through other Christians to correct us, too (Prov 3:12). We went "cold turkey" after that, and did not have sex again until the day after we were married. It was a difficult adjustment, but it was worth it. It gave us the opportunity to concentrate on the premarital counseling we were receiving from the associate pastor of our church. It also gave us time to work on our prayer life, and to read the Bible and to understand how a Christian married couple is supposed to handle themselves. The wonderful result was that before we got married, it was just sex. After we got married, and to this very day, it is making love!

Some have even lost their lives because they allowed themselves to enter into a sexually inappropriate relationship, only to wind up murdered by the other person, or a person or persons who were associated with the other person. Prisons are full of people serving lengthy sentences for "crimes of passion." The book of Proverbs talks about this matter, using a possible and realistic consequence of adultery:

> But a man who commits adultery has no sense; whoever
> does so destroys himself. Blows and disgrace are his lot,
> and his shame will never be wiped away. For jealousy

arouses a husband's fury, and he will show no mercy when he takes revenge. He will not accept any compensation; he will refuse a bribe, however great it is. (Prov 6:32–35)

Back in my "backsliding" days, there were times that I would rent and watch pornographic movies. I used to envy the guys who were getting to have sex with so many beautiful women: then the AIDS epidemic hit the world scene, and the adult film industry did not escape the onslaught. Many of those same guys I envied, or females I fantasized about, ended up being infected with the virus. Others were apparently distraught over an unhappy life, and committed suicide. The best biblical example I can think about is my previous reference to King Solomon. As I stated before, he had access to literally hundreds of women and had a lot of sex. He probably had as much sex or more sex with women than a modern-day adult film star. Yet even in the midst of all that, after the Lord God telling him how disappointed he was in him because he allowed himself to turn away from him, he finally got to the point where he saw that entire sort of thing as, in his words, "meaningless" (Eccl 1:14). He finally came to realize that serving the Lord God was *the* act that gave his life meaning, and not the women, the riches, and the other stuff. King Solomon's example really made me think. Although the Lord God admonished him for his behavior, he still made it clear to Solomon that he loved him and that it wasn't too late for him to change his ways and refocus his mind and his actions on him. He did this by allowing Solomon to hang onto his kingdom for the rest of his life (1 Kgs 11:12).

The situation that Solomon went through made me think about how so many Christian men in today's society are bombarded by sexual imagery in the media, with its messages that attempt to sell the false belief that creating a modern-day harem makes them a social success. Brothers, there are none of you who can name a single man on this planet who had access to the kind of worldly pleasures King Solomon had before he realized the futility of world's sexual offerings outside the marriage bed.

Now, if that is not enough to convince you, think about born-again Christian men who were once adult film actors, such as the late Harry Reems, or former professional athletes such as Deion Sanders, Darryl Strawberry, and George Foreman; men who now make it clear that premarital sex and other worldly pleasures are meaningless compared to their relationship with the Lord God, Jesus Christ and the Holy Spirit! Brothers, if you've ever heard other Christian men who have "been there and done that," when it comes to the so-called "player" lifestyle, and they tell you there's nothing to benefit from it, so don't even bother to try; believe them!

Let's look at Joseph, who in the midst of being sold into slavery to the Egyptian Potiphar knew of the importance of not giving into temptation. Assigned to run his master's household, Joseph was continually sexually harassed and propositioned by Potiphar's wife. He continued to refuse to sleep with her until one day she grabbed him to make her request perfectly clear. Joseph did the right thing; he ran away from Potiphar's wife (Gen 39:12). The Bible tells us that we must "flee" fornication (1 Cor 6:18). Although Potiphar's wife falsely accused him of rape, resulting in his false imprisonment, Joseph's choice would eventually result in the Lord God blessing him tremendously. Now here's someone who goes from being sold into slavery, and sent to prison unjustly, but eventually becomes the second most powerful man in the most powerful empire of the time (Gen 41:41)! Now that's the Lord God's favor! And this is all because he made correct decisions, such as not committing adultery. Former professional football player Deion Sanders, of whom I mentioned earlier, spoke along these same lines. He said that it got to the point where the access to beautiful women, and having frequent sex with them, lost its luster, and he found that he needed something much more. It was his accepting Jesus Christ as his personal Lord and Savior that finally gave his life meaning; not the glitter and gleam of professional sports superstardom.[4] Think about it. Even though one of Shakespeare's

---

4. Deion Sanders came to my church, Empowerment Temple AME Church, Dr. Jamal H. Bryant, pastor, sometime after he retired in 2005. I don't remember the Sunday he spoke, but my wife, Karen, and I were in attendance.

characters in a play said "all that glitters is not gold" and it's not in the Bible, that still makes sense, doesn't it?[5] What *is* in the Bible is that we are not supposed to allow ourselves to be led into temptation (Matt 6:13), and that we must love wisdom enough to the point where we don't allow lust to kill us spiritually, and physically.

Here's another personal example that I hope you can relate to. Once again, in my single days, many of which were backsliding days, my friends and cousins would frequently talk about how cool it would be to go down to Rio De Janerio, Brazil, for Carnival. We fantasized about going down there with a box of condoms, and making sure that box was empty by the time it was time to get back on the plane to go home. We had seen pornography where the Brazilian women in the scenes, as well as the ones shown in footage on the beaches, were the most beautiful we had ever seen. I had always been too broke during my single days to go to Rio. I can afford to go now, but I seriously doubt that I will ever go there now. I definitely will *never* go there without my wife by my side. My going down to Rio alone would be the biggest mistake of my life, due to the unbelievable temptation that would be all around me. As long as I stay away from Rio, I will stay away from temptation. Wherever it is that you know is one that would be too tempting for you to go without your wife, or go without being sexually inappropriate, you need to stay away from that place. It might even be the massage parlor or the strip club across town, or the night club downtown. Yeah, that's right. You can even get sex from some strippers for the right price. And you can find one-night stands if you hang around the club long enough. And you can catch the same hellish fallout from the same bad decisions in those places, too. The same rule applies: if you want to do right, you must stay away from places where you will be tempted to do wrong. The same King Solomon who had previously engaged in so much lustful activity that led him away from the Lord God had the foresight, knowledge and common sense, and therefore, wisdom

---

The appearance was taped for a latter UPN broadcast and was at one time available on YouTube, but it no longer appears to be available online.

5. Shakespeare, *Merchant of Venice*, act 2, scene 7.

to forewarn his own son. We see this evidence in the Bible, where he tells his son not to lust in his heart after the beauty of a woman who would lead him astray (Prov 6:25). He warns his son not to be taken in by the seductive words of an adulteress (Prov 7:5, 6–27), nor should he allow himself to give in to the influence of a prostitute (Prov 6:26). It is a powerfully dangerous thing that we must avoid. How many people we know or know about have ruined their professional and family lives due to inappropriate sexual relations either without being married or outside of their marriage? Is it really worth it? We're talking about several minutes of pleasure for a lifetime of pain and regret! Men of the Lord God; we must think through this, pause and avoid the trap of lust through fornication, because at the end of the day, what you thought what felt so good and was so good for you, really turned out to be something unbelievably spiritually unhealthy for you. Once again, let's look at and take the Apostle Paul's advice. If we really cannot contain ourselves when it comes to this problem, let's ask the Lord to prepare us for marriage. If we cannot control ourselves in this part of our lives, let's pray to the Lord to introduce us to our wife, and prepare us to be the best monogamous, kind, loving husband we can be. This way, when it comes to sex, we will no longer burn with desire for other women; all of that pent-up sexual energy will be reserved for our fine, spirit-filled wonderful wife (1 Cor 7:9)! This is what I do. Any sexual arousal I experience is something I transfer into acceptable arousal. What do I mean by that? I mean that *any* time I experience sexual arousal, I can engage in the spiritual self-defense of the kind in which the *only* female I will express that arousal with through intercourse will be with my loving wife! That is a very powerful form of spiritual self-defense! No matter what image, for example, of the opposite sex that by chance, arouses me, whether it is a commercial with sexy images of the opposite sex, or entering an "innocent" public place like a shopping mall or a swimming pool during the hot summer months (you would have to be blind not to at least notice what you will see, whether you like it or not, even if you're not looking intentionally), we can make sure that our wife, or future wife can benefit from the energetic expression of this situation. For you unmarried men, I encourage you to do the same thing. Although you have to wait longer than those of us who are already married, you will find that it's worth it, because on your honeymoon night, your wife will appreciate the unleashing of all of that powerful energy! Take my word for that! The woman who the Lord God has blessed you with as your wife will greatly appreciate your energetic expression of the sex act in a bed that is pure and undefiled!

So, here's your final advice, regarding this spiritual self-defense lesson. It is important that you practice these techniques; it's the only way you're going to get them right.

- Remember that Bible says that you must steer clear of lustful activity (1 Cor 6:18–20). If you are tempted, literally run away from the situation. I am serious about this. There are Christian men who would still be alive today if they had done this. It may sound weird, but what is worse; you doing something that feels weird to you, or dying? You make the choice; just make sure it's the right choice.

- Seek the help and advice of other Christian men who are willing to talk to you, who have overcome the sin and temptation of fornication, and now lead spiritually productive lives. Seek a person who has overcome the specific type of premarital sexual sin in which you are struggling.

- Stay away from visual material that results in your being tempted to engage in lustful actions. This does not only mean pornography, but any media online in books and magazines, and on the television set that would result in the temptation.

Chapter 7

Signing the Peace Treaty

Using Examples of Strong Christian Married Men to Foster a Successful Relationship with Your Wife or Future Wife

BROTHERS, I BELIEVE THAT when it comes to many if not most of us, if we were taught to respect others, and had a good nurturing relationship with our parents, we were taught to respect all people, especially women. However, too many guys, some of them who profess to be Christians, are not applying the Golden Rule when it comes to how we treat women; we're not treating many of them the way we want to be treated. Recently, a popular R&B recording artist was accused of allegedly assaulting his equally popular recording artist girlfriend. Before the assault occurred, he admitted on a popular television show that he grew up witnessing his father physically abuse his mother. I believe that a significantly large number of misguided males who are domestic abusers have seen other males in their family be abusive, too. Many of these males might have been victims of some kind of abuse themselves.

Now at the same time, I realize that there are some women who are verbally, and even physically abusive to men. In his book *Makes Me Wanna Holler*, journalist Nathan McCall talks about the physical abuse he suffered from his first wife. He, like I, was raised to never put one's hands on a woman in anger, no matter the situation. I have had two situations in my life, where, in the midst of a verbal disagreement, a woman with whom I was in a relationship put their hands on me in an inappropriate way. In both of those situations, I ended those relationships shortly thereafter. Any woman who experiences the same thing should also leave the relationship. For any of you who are abusers, you are not following the Lord God's word, nor are you following the Lord God's will. The Golden Rule is biblical; it tells us to treat others the way we want to be treated (Luke 6:31). We must treat our wives and future wives the way we want to be treated.

If we in turn are doing this and not getting it in return, then Christian counseling, through a pastor, for example, or a Christian therapist is a great alternative. The Bible instructs is this way: Do your best to present yourself to the Lord God as one approved, a worker who does not need to be ashamed and who correctly handles the word of truth" (2 Tim 2:15). In addition, Jesus reminded us that we are to be the type of people who go the extra mile (Matt 5:41), which also goes for our relationships. Does that go both ways? No doubt. Yet, you want to make sure you're doing your part.

Another sticking point between Christian men and women in relationships is communication. More often than not, we don't really know how to get through to each other. I strongly recommend that you read *The Five Love Languages: How to Express Heartfelt Commitment to Your Mate*, by Gary Chapman. In the book, Chapman emphasizes that everyone has a love language, or more than one love language. In fact, there are five key love languages: words of affirmation, quality time, receiving gifts, acts of service, and physical touch. My wife, Karen, and I take the process of knowing each other's love languages seriously. As I mentioned previously we have been happily married for over fifteen years. Right away, in the beginning of our relationship, I shared with her this book, and explained the love languages to her. I found out that her key love languages are as follows: acts of service, quality time, and receiving gifts. She knows that my key love languages are words of affirmation, physical touch, and quality time. For her, acts of service are at the top of the list, while my number one love language is words of affirmation. At the writing of this chapter, I was compelled to stop writing and actually call my wife from work, and double-check this with her. I found that I still knew her top three love languages, and was also motivated to satisfy her number one love language by writing a "honey do" list for the summer. As I asked her over the phone the key things she wanted me to accomplish for her this summer, the list resulted in thirteen items. I really felt good about putting that list together. I could also tell by the sound of her voice, that she was pleased that I called to place the deserved high priority on her love language. Brothers, my point is that we must learn how to speak the love language of our mate. This has to be the highest priority. At the same time, it is a two-way street. Make sure you are in a relationship where your wife or future wife is also doing their part to learn *your* love language, too! It can't be one sided; two people are in the relationship or marriage, and two people must be proactive about communicating effectively with one another.

Also, in addition to reading *The Five Love* Languages, I would encourage every Christian man who is married and who is going to be married to read two books: Eric Wilson, Steven Kendrick, and Alex Kendrick's book, *Fireproof*, and Stephen Kendrick and Alex Kendrick's book *The Love Dare*. *Fireproof* is the story of Caleb Holt, a dedicated firefighter. Although he is an excellent and well-respected man, regarding his profession, his marriage is on the rocks. He and his wife, Catherine, are drifting apart: neither seems to understand each other's daily work stresses and pressures, his firefighter's job and her hospital administrator's job. Their marriage continues to unravel to the point where they have had enough, and are ready to get a divorce. Caleb's father, sensing that there is trouble in the marriage, strongly suggests that Caleb reads and follows the instructions in the book *The Love Dare*; a book that saved his and Caleb's mother's marriage. He reluctantly decides to do so. He finds that the book is a forty-day practice, in which a married couple goes through exercises designed to show them how to practice lifelong unconditional love. After reading the book, and following its instructions, the power of the Lord, working through the book transforms his and his wife's thinking, and their life. The book became a successful and powerful motion picture as well, starring Kirk Cameron and Erin Bethea.

Brothers, I strongly encourage you to buy and read all three books and rent the *Fireproof* DVD. Remember: in order to have a good, strong, Christian marriage, we must follow the blueprints that, in the body of Christ, are placed before us. The Lord God works through Christian brothers such as Kirk Cameron, Eric Wilson, and the Kendrick brothers through their ministries and the success of their marriages. Other great examples such as the late Reverend Billy Graham, Bishop T. D. Jakes, Rev. Joel Osteen, and Rev. Dr. Fred K. C. Price also stand as examples of strong Christian men who are great examples of equally strong Christian husbands. Let's pattern our marriage or future marriage after these warriors for Christ.

We must also remember that love is a decision. The romantic part, the courting, and the physical part are all exciting parts of the process, but that decisive love, that agape love, is the love that makes a marriage last; the unconditional love you feel for each other, and the unconditional love that Jesus feels for you both. Be willing to always keep the lines of communication open, continually working on being the best example of "one flesh" (Mark 10:18) that you can possibly be. Remember: marriage is a "*we*" thing, not a "*me*" thing. It's one of the toughest jobs you'll ever love, and the dividends pay off daily; you really get out of it what you put into it.

It still amazes my wife and me that the a research study once revealed that the average married couple spends only ten minutes a week talking to each other. Ten minutes! No Christian married couple should be in that statistic, because no Christian married couple is average. We have the supernatural power of the Lord God that enables us to accomplish much more than we can on our own. The problems occur when Christian married couples lean unto their own understanding and don't seek the kingdom of the Lord God first (Prov 3:5–6). The enemy can come on in and put stupid thoughts in our head, resulting in even more foolish things coming out of our mouths. We must be careful to think, and especially pray when it comes to everything that involves our marriage. We cannot take this for granted. Remember: we are at war, and the enemy, along with trying to take everything else from you, is trying to steal from, kill, and destroy your marriage (John 10:10). Remember, even in your marriage, that you must resist the devil so that he will flee from you (James 4:7).

Brothers, when it comes to consuming mass media, I also encourage you to careful and discerning, regarding what you're listening to and what you're viewing. Too much of what we're seeing and hearing in global mass media is not glorifying the beauty and sanctity of marriage. It seems as though much of the media is glorifying every other type of lifestyle other than marriage, or advocating extramarital affairs of every type. I was turning the channels recently when I stumbled upon a film on one of the movie channels. I pressed the information key on my remote, only to find that the film was about couples who were in unfulfilling marriages, who had decided to have an "open" marriage where they could see other people of the opposite sex. I immediately changed the channel because I did not want information like that to enter my brain space. I encourage you to do likewise. It does not matter whether or not you believe that you are strong enough not to follow examples like this once you encounter them on television, or the internet, in books, on the radio, and in other types of media. The fact of the matter is this: anything that tries to negatively influence you, even in a subtle, darn near subliminal way, is of the enemy, and not of the Lord. We have to be very careful. We must remember that our enemy is a deceptive, slick liar who works through people who don't even know that they're being used by him (John 8:44). Don't just let anything go up into your head, and don't ever let your guard down! Remember that it's the enemy's job to attempt to wreak havoc in your marriage. The Bible warn us not to "give the devil a foothold" (Eph 4:27). We must remember that we serve an omnipotent, omnipresent, and omniscient the Lord God who has already defeated the enemy and his principalities. We have this power of the Lord God, and we must remember to have that armor on at all times, and the blood of Jesus, and use this against the enemy. These are some of the best tactics you can use to apply spiritual self-defense to your marriage.

Brothers, the next spiritual self-defense advice I have for you is the following:

- Purchase and read *The Love Dare*. Follow the forty-day journey to a more fulfilling marriage. This book is for married couples only.

- Purchase and read *The Five Love Languages: How to Express Heartfelt Commitment to Your Mate*. It is extremely important that you and your mate know each other's love language *now*, especially before you get married.

- Spend quality time with Christian married couples who you know have great, long, sustaining marriages. If they are willing to do so, ask these couples about their relationship with the Lord, and how it has resulted in their marital success.

- Put aside at least thirty minutes communication time per day for you and your mate. Turn the TV, cell phone and any other electronic device off, and give each other your undivided attention. Ask her what kind of day she had. Be sincerely interested in her problems, concerns, and triumphs of the day. Listen without interruption, and don't try to be a "Mr. Fix-It." Women want and value your time and attention more than your proposed solution.

Chapter 8

Learning How to Really Love Yourself
Killing the Low Self-Esteem Demon

IF THERE IS ONE key problem I see in this country today, that is low self-esteem. Being university faculty, I see the symptoms in too many students. When that one or two students in each of my classes displays inappropriate behavior in the form of not following class rules stated in my syllabus, or has an unproductive attitude toward learning, many times I can actually find that they are also exhibiting the same unproductive attitude outside of the classroom. Many of my "problem" students or "diamonds in the rough students" (I believe they all are diamonds), are just as intelligent as the ones who are doing well. Yet, I have learned from some very reliable sources that there have been those who have struggled and continue to struggle with low-self-esteem-related issues and behavior. I continue to have students who struggle with broken homes, fatherlessness, scars from physical and sexual abuse, witnessing the violent deaths of loved ones by homicide or losing them to suicide, and even, in some cases, their own attempts to commit suicide. In the past I've also have had students struggle with getting into trouble with law enforcement, even while they were students. I have found that all I can do is show unconditional agape love for them, pray for them, encourage them, and constantly remind them that they are great human beings who have what it takes to be successful in anything they want to do in life. It concerns me greatly that too many of my students seem to be teetering between a positive and a negative direction, and I believe it has to do with many of them struggling with low self-esteem issues.

I'm convinced that more people must learn to love, first loving the person looking back at them in the mirror. I believe that the greatest human problem in the world today is low self-esteem, and I believe that there are a number of Christians dealing with this problem as well. Jesus said that we must love the Lord, and our neighbor as ourselves (Matt 22:37–39). How can a person do this if they don't love themselves? I believe that most human misery begins with a self-imposed loathing of oneself that began as a result of some type of learned behavior from others, be it parents or other family members, peers, and just the general environment. How do we stop the enemy's plan to infect generation after generation with self-hatred? First, I believe we must begin with ourselves. Yes, I said the beginning point begins with us. We as Christian men must examine our own behavior, and honestly ask ourselves this question: are we behaving in a loving way toward ourselves and others? I have witness too many men who are Christians, who struggle with the love test. They claim to love other human beings, but feel they have to be in some type of unhealthy competition against other men. That Christian male athlete who delivers cheap shots and engages in vicious trash talk to his opponents, the Christian male who abuses and disrespects his spouse, and the Christian male who engages in any form of road rage: in order to turn things around, I'm convinced that they must immerse themselves into 1 Corinthians 13, the Love Chapter, if they are to work toward the path of truly being loving human beings and a real men. That's right, brothers. A real man is a man who loves himself, his neighbor, and demonstrates it daily.

The next spiritual self-defense technique I'm going to emphasize to you is the most important; mastering the act of continually engaging in unconditional love toward all. So let's begin with looking at the process of loving ourselves. Brothers, this is not going to happen for you until you really, truly realize, who you are in the body of Christ. You must understand that you are fearfully and wonderfully made (Ps 139:14). You must realize that you are the righteousness of the Lord God in Christ Jesus (2 Cor 5:21). You must realize that you are made in the Lord God's image (Gen 1:27), that you are the head and not the tail (Deut 28:13), and that you are a royal priesthood (1 Pet 2:9) with a body that is a temple (1 Cor 6:19–20) that needs to be taken care of! You are an heir to all the wonderful promises of good health and prosperity that was promised to and given to Abraham himself (Gen 12:1–3)! So with that in mind, how *dare* you have low self-esteem! In order to realize how great you are, you must love yourself, and therefore, *act* like the great man you are! A great man does not cheat on his wife. A great man does not lie, cheat, or steal. A great man does not engage in lustful activity. A great man adds value to his community and does not take away from it. A great man raises the children he brings into the world. A great man is an others-centered man who works to add value to the lives of others. And finally, a great man in the kingdom of God and the body of Christ is not perfect, far from it, but daily works on his spiritual self-defense to prevent the acts I've just mentioned from happening.

Brothers, I believe that a huge amount of misery in this world has been caused by people who have low-self-esteem, with a lot of them being males. Abusive behavior is a key example, historically, and in the present day. I will never forget hearing on the radio one day that 90 percent of American prison inmates experienced some type of abuse in their lives before winding up incarcerated. I found recently that 40 percent of male prison inmates were sexually abused as children.[1] The most horrendous example of this fact is that two of the greatest mass murderers history has ever known were physically abused as children. I am talking about Adolf Hitler and Josef Stalin. Caligula, one of the most despicable and tyrannical emperors of ancient Rome, was regularly sexually abused as a

---

1. See Fondacaro, "Psychological Impact of Childhood Sexual Abuse," 361–69.

little boy by his uncle, the emperor Tiberius. I believe that childhood abuse plays into this problem, too.

If a significant portion of male prison inmates in the United States are victims of some type of abuse, either physically, sexually, or psychologically *before even being sent to prison*, then I believe that whatever crime or crimes they committed were out of a demonic spirit of low self-esteem based on what was done to them. Now, from the world's standards, I have no statistical proof of this offhand, but I have better proof; the Bible says it! Again, if we don't love our neighbor as ourselves, that means we don't love ourselves, and we don't give a rip about our neighbor (Matt 22:37–39).

You don't believe me? Look at all human conflict taking place in the world right now, such as wars, for example. The root of war is a result of people, usually men, not loving themselves, and therefore, not loving their neighbor. Did I say "men?" I meant to say "males," because a *real* man loves himself and his neighbor. Brothers, it's time to *man up* and be a man! Study the Bible and find what it takes to love you, love others, and be a *real* man in the body of Christ! This is the most powerful spiritual self-defense tactic!

So, the key is studying and application (2 Tim 2:15). It is not enough to just pick up your Bible and read 1 Corinthians 13; you must live it! We as men in the body of Christ must hold each other accountable, regarding working on being more loving human beings. And brothers, I must tell you, it's a daily struggle for me, too when it comes to certain things. When someone cuts me off in traffic and something mean comes out of my mouth as a result, I immediately as the Lord to forgive my corrupt communication. I also take Dr. Bill Winston's advice, and say aloud, "I cancel that," when anything mean, vicious, or hateful comes out of my mouth that's directed toward others when driving my car, or in any other situation.[2]

You see, this learning to love thing is a constant work in progress. You must work on it every day. It is important to not only seek the mentorship of other Christian men who are good at loving themselves and others, it is important to seek those whose

2. See Winston, *Law of Confession*.

previous tests can be examples that you should follow. For example, I remember Dr. Creflo Dollar's extraordinary testimony about a situation in which the Lord God allowed him to go through a major test, regarding demonstrating love in the midst of a person who was acting very unlovable. On a rare day off, he and Taffi, his wife, went to an early movie matinee. During the film's showing, he remembered that he had to take his medicine at a certain time. He used the light from his silenced cell phone to check the time. All of a sudden, he felt the hard jab of a finger hitting his shoulder. He turned around to find that an elderly man was sitting there. He angrily commented on the phone being a distraction while he was trying to see the film. Dr. Dollar stated that he is from the school of thought where, from a fleshly point of view, someone who touches him that way is subject to being in a fistfight. Yet, he remembered that he is commanded by the Lord God to not only love this person, but to not return evil with evil, but to return evil with love. He responded by not acting out in the flesh, but acting in the spirit. I thank the Lord God for Dr. Dollar's great example. Dr. Dollar did not indicate what he said to the man, if he said anything at all, but he did say that he handled the situation with love, and in a spiritual way, and not by the flesh. I'm not saying that I would have handled that situation in the flesh, and I pray that I would have handled it in love, the way Dr. Dollar did. Dr. Dollar's point is clear: to obey the Lord God by loving ourselves and our neighbor is to love the Lord God.[3] To deny the Lord God's word regarding love and anything else is to deny self and engage in a self-centered love for ourselves that is not the Lord God's version of our loving ourselves. Having a Lord God-centered love for ourselves is totally different from a self-centered, selfish self-love: a self-centered love is contrary to the Lord God. Remember; this is biblical. A man who practices love does not get into needless arguments and confrontations. A *real* man in the body of Christ remembers that there are a lot of hurting people out there who are in such pain that they

3. This is from a sermon my wife, Karen, and I attended in March 2008. Dr. Dollar was the guest pastor at Victory Christian Ministries International, where the pastors are Tony and Cynthia Brazelton (Suitland, MD).

are depressed, and are full of rage and low self-esteem. Many of these people have *rarely or never* experienced acts of love directed their way.

Therefore, it is important that we are always working on our spiritual self-defense so that we can handle all situations in love, making sure it is that others-centered, nonjudgmental, and all-encompassing, no-strings-attached love. This kind of love only comes with practice; not by turning it on or off like a water faucet. This kind of love is known as an agape love; a love that is expressed to everyone in every situation, no matter what that situation happens to be. Here's how we can practice that love. Let's go to the Bible and look at the book of 1 Corinthians, chapter 13, look at what it says about love, and let's use this for your most important spiritual self-defense move, regarding your training.

In summary, the first three verses of this chapter tells us that we can have many creative and useful talents, be a very knowledgeable human being, and perform other-centered tasks in our community; and all of it won't matter if we are not loving people (1 Cor 13:1–3). That makes sense, doesn't it? You and I can think of people who were and are in the public eye, as well as people we know who are this way. They are very talented and intelligent, and have the potential to do great things, yet they stifle themselves because they don't love themselves, and, as a result, don't show love to others. Think about that creative artist who is and abusive spouse. Think about that world-class athlete who is always in trouble with the law. Think about that movie star or comedian who died from a drug overdose. You really don't have to look farther than your own community, and many times your own family. You know someone who could be doing great things in their lives, yet, for some reason, they have allowed low self-esteem and hatred of others to allow themselves to become stagnant and unproductive human beings. Take love out of the equation, and everything falls apart. When I think about this example, the A&E show *Intervention* comes to mind. The show's premise centers upon the process in which a person with an addiction is filmed over a period of several days. The person believes that he or she is being filmed for a documentary on addiction. They are really being prepared for the day when he or she is unknowingly led to a room where their family and an addiction specialist meets them in a room, and gives them the choice to either go to a rehabilitation center that day, or depart from their lives forever. During the course of the show, we see the individuals engaging in self-destructive behavior. Yet, the most striking thing that we find within the first several minutes of the show is what triggered their addiction in the first place. A black screen appears with white letters, explaining what major incident in their life probably triggered their self-hatred, and ultimately, their addiction. Many of those who choose treatment learn coping skills, the greatest one being the process of learning to love themselves, either for the first time, or the first time in a long time. Not everyone in the show accepts treatment, nor do they complete their prescribed treatment program. Those who do complete their program are shown in a follow-up sequence within the last several minutes of the show. Many times the key things they talk about, regarding their recovery, are newly learned self-love concepts.

The fourth verse of this chapter really breaks it down as to how someone can display low self-esteem and hatred toward others by being impatient, unkind, envious, and boastful (1 Cor 13:4). I know and you know too, people who are constantly impatient. Impatience is not an act of love. I believe that many, if not most people who are impatient have occasional momentary lapses, when it comes to impatience. Yet, someone who constantly displays this characteristic is not showing practicing the action of being a loving human being, and that, in of itself, is a problem. Anyone who is not working to become a more patient person is not interested in working toward being a loving person.

When it comes to lack of kindness, I believe that is a more obvious example. The most unkind people you will hear about or run into are people who are hateful, first to themselves, and to other people. Many times you will see signs, in addition to their unkind treatment of others. They could engage in some kind of substance abuse, legally or illegally. They could be morbidly obese, which could be an indication more about *what's eating them* instead of what they're eating. They could be a product of a broken home or an abusive relationship. Whatever the case may be, a heart filled with love is what they need in order to not be that way. I would even place rudeness in this same category, if the person is consciously and knowingly being rude, and not used to have these character defects, who now, rarely display these due to asking the Lord God to give them a heart full of love.

I also challenge you to take a person, any person, who is boastful and full of pride, and they probably experienced something in their lives that is a result of their feeling that they have to put on a mask to cover up true feelings of low self-esteem. They could be masking some type of pain, and they are carrying on in such a way to veer others away from the truth, the real heart of the matter. If you are displaying these behaviors, be honest with yourself and think about whether or not the lack of loving yourself is a primary reason for this behavior. If this is the case, remember that you can learn to love yourself and others, and this chapter is the key to understanding that process. Be transparent and honest with the Lord God and yourself. The scripture makes it very clear that the *only* boasting we're supposed to be doing is boasting in the Lord, and talking about his goodness, grace, mercy and love (1 Cor 1:31)!

The chapter's next verse reminds us that love isn't rude or easily angered, nor does it keep a record of wrongs (1 Cor 13:5). I believe that in order to be a truly loving person, we must treat others the way we want to be treated (Matt 7:12) which means not being rude to others. When we make the decision to not be rude to others, this shows that we are sincerely showing them love and kindness. Also, show me a person who is easily angered, and I'll show you a person who has difficultly loving himself and others, and who has additional difficulties in his life do to this problem. All you have to do is turn on any law enforcement-related reality show like *Cops* and you will usually see people who act this way in handcuffs being escorted to the back of a police car. Have you also noticed that most of the time, when you see people act this way, they are grown adults who are so full of anger and rage to the point where they're having a childish temper tantrum? They may have not been exposed to the Love Chapter scripture that is a reminder to grown adults to put away childish things (1 Cor 13:11). Understand that you *never* engage in spiritual self-defense without engaging in love; love for yourself and your fellow human beings, no matter what the enemy wants to see you engaged in low self-esteem and every negative thing associated with it. He wants to see you ruin relationships with others and lose everything that is important to you, by sowing hatred and poor conduct into your life.

We must always remember, as I emphasized previously, that when you practice and perfect the spiritual self-defense tactic of love, you continue to learn the most powerful spiritual self-defense move possible. Why? Because this chapter tells us that it is a fool-proof tactic. The eighth verse of this chapter reminds us that love *never* fails (1 Cor 13:8)! You should be fired up to know that! The Lord God is telling us through the Apostle Paul, that if we constantly practice this spiritual self-defense technique, the greatest one of all, that we will always be successful when using it!

As I wrote this information, I did so on Martin Luther King Day. What a great example of success, regarding the use of this tactic! Make no mistake: Dr. King was a master of this spiritual self-defense technique. Look at all the good Dr. King accomplished merely by showing love; love for his enemies, his community, and for his Lord God! I think about how Mahatma Gandhi, a major influence on Dr. King, used love for his enemies and love for his people to free the entire country of India! Most of all, I think about how the Lord God loved this world so much, that he sent his only Son, our Lord and Savior Jesus (John 3:16), who showed the world what love is truly about, when he died on the cross and shed his blood for the world's sins; all out of an unconditional and unfailing love. The last verse of this chapter emphasizes the importance of having faith, hope, and love, with love being the greatest of the three (1 Cor 13:13). We see right there that this is proof that this is the most important and greatest spiritual self-defense technique that we have! We must hone this skill to a knife edge. The great self-defense artists, such as the late Bruce Lee, Jet Li, Jackie Chan, Tony Jaa, and Iko Uwais were and are known for their self-discipline, their devotion to their way of life, and their mastery of the martial arts. The body of Christ has to have strong loving men who are masters at spiritual self-defense, especially the mastery of love, in order for there to be a revival of the expression of true love in this world!

The more I live, the more I realize that many men struggle with the importance of self-love; the first form of love that they must accomplish. I must emphasize this again: the Bible tells us to love our neighbor, or our fellow human beings, as we love ourselves. The Lord God tells us that this commandment is second only to loving him (Matt 22:37–40). I believe that many men, especially a lot of young men, don't realize that the Lord God, their father in heaven loves them so much, and wants them to get their lives together and follow him to the point that he makes it clear that each man should realize that there is greatness in them (Eph 1:18). The Lord God loves us so much that he wants us to break out of the bondage of low self-esteem and pride that result in the downfall of many men in our society.

Since August 2012 I have lived in South Carolina. The Lord has blessed me with the opportunity to lead a men's Bible study at my church, Williams Chapel African Methodist Episcopal Church. I have noticed that most of the men are elderly retirees. At fifty-five years of age, I am one of the youngest attendees. Although I am thankful for the brothers who do come to the Bible study on a regular basis, I am in prayer for and speaking into existence an anticipation of a harvest of young men who are hungry to grow in their Christian walk. Although it has yet to happen, I believe that this will happen, and when it does, it will be a wonderful thing to behold. One of our church's former pastors, Rev. Dr. Caesar R. Richburg, gave me permission to address the men in the congregation. Before my speech, I prayed that the Lord would place on my heart the right things to say; things that will make sense to and connect to men in the congregation, especially those younger men without the proper guidance, who need to know who they are and whose they are in the body of Christ. When I talked to them on that warm, sunny Sunday morning, I spoke along these lines: I told them that just like the saying, "there's an app for that," referring to their smart phones, I wanted them to realize that whatever they are going through in their lives, there's a verse of scripture for that. I said to them that the Bible has all the answers for them, and that their Heavenly Father is there for them to lead them and guide them, even if, for instance, their biological father was not there to do so. I told them that the Bible says that we're not supposed to forsake the assembling of ourselves together (Heb 10:25). I emphasized that as it applies to church, it also applies to Bible study. I said that the enemy doesn't want men to come together that way, and that we need to do it anyway just to give an already-defeated devil a nervous breakdown. I said that when men in the body of Christ get together and study together and learn together, there is nothing they can't accomplish. I told them that the book of Deuteronomy states that the Lord God wants us to have the blessings and not the curses. (Deut 28). I concluded my speech my letting the men know that I look forward to seeing them at men's Bible study next week. I also said, "Let's fellowship together, let's learn together, let's do great things together in the body of Christ, and let's take our rightful place as spiritually educated, strong Christian men in our communities!" Afterward I prayed that the Lord would instill in their hearts a spirit of urgency to grow spiritually through the collective act of attending the men's Bible study.

During the course of this time, I have pondered the reason why more men have not attended the men's Bible study. I believe that too many men are wearing this rough, false exterior that is a defense mechanism to hide the fear and the doubt they have about themselves. A few years ago, I remember being blessed with viewing one of Pastor Joel Osteen's sermons. In this sermon, he emphasized that researchers who are experts in genetics have found that we are predestined to take on good and bad physical and personality characteristics of our parents, grandparents and previous generations. At the same time, he also mentioned that researchers have found that *epigenetics* exists. This literally means "on top of the genes." Researchers found that there are certain negative genes that we can literally learn to "deactivate" and not pass down to future generations. This is great news! When Pastor Osteen recently revealed this information to me, it steeled me with an even stronger resolve. He emphasized that once we deactivate these negative genes with the guidance of the Lord, we put a stop to the passing of these genes to future generations. Osteen also emphasized that we can activate positive genes that can be passed down to our own future generations, and that we don't stop the negative ones, they can affect our future generations for years to come.[4] I believe that so many of the men in our congregation and community are dealing with some type of negative gene that has been passed down to them. The following week, when I held Bible study the men who were there at the Bible study and I spoke about how many of these young men are letting pride get in the way of coming to our Bible study. All of the younger men in the church know about our Bible study, but only a few have attended. We also discussed the fact that many of these men, even those in the church, don't realize the greatness that the Lord God has already placed inside them. If they really knew how great they were, they would be coming to our Bible study in droves just so they could understand how to access the wonder-working power of the Lord God inside them that can result in their realizing their greatness, and do a powerful work in the Lord God's kingdom.

At the same time, we could only lament the fact that we see the mug shots of too many young adult males in the area where we live who are in trouble with the law. We discussed a recent occurrence, one in which on another university campus in the state, in an ongoing dispute, one misguided male student killed another male student. Apparently, the young man who allegedly shot him had been in an ongoing dispute with him. The feud reached an irrevocable boiling point when on a sunny Friday afternoon, the misguided young man and four of his friends confronted the other

4. This information is from a sermon from Joel Osteen's weekly television broadcast. I don't remember the date; however, I remember its positive impact for my bolstering my spiritual self-defense techniques.

young man, a popular student who was on the university's football team. In the midst of a heated argument, the young man at the center of the dispute with the student pulled out a gun and shot him in the neck, mortally wounding him. I think about how one innocent young man, who had a promising future ahead of him, was taken from this world much too soon. Also, I think about the alleged assailant who, because of pride and an unwillingness to refrain from engaging in a deadly confrontation, has irrevocably ruined his chance of having a productive future. I believe that if the misguided young males, especially the assailant, knew of their greatness, and did not resort to pride, that confrontation never would have happened. I am convinced that the four misguided young males had very little or no knowledge at all about the greatness that the Lord God had put inside of them. I believe that there are thousands, perhaps millions of men all over this country and the world who wouldn't do most of the irresponsible and negative stuff they do if they only knew the greatness that the Lord God has already placed inside them.

In the book of Exodus, the Lord God reassures a reluctant and unconvinced Moses that he has already provided the greatness that is inside of him to lead his people out of slavery (Exod 4:1–7). Although Moses was doubtful of his abilities, he did not lose his faith. The Lord God revealed victory after victory, showing Moses that what he said was true, and that it would come to pass. Brothers, it is my prayer that more of you would realize just how the Lord God sees you and not how the world may see you. The Lord God sees your greatness, and he wants to bring it out of you. You just have to have the willingness to step out on faith, and walk into the blessings that he has already placed before you.

Are you ready to continue the journey to earn your "black belt" in spiritual self-defense? Well, if your answer is "yes," here is what you must do:

- Read 1 Corinthians 13 for yourself. Seek a Christian mentor you trust, such as a minister or your pastor, who is farther advanced than you in applying unconditional love in your Christian walk. He or she will monitor your progress, regarding whether or not you understand the chapter. Remember: in order for you to master this, the greatest spiritual self-defense technique of all, you must make sure you understand the instructions.

- Read through the books of Matthew, Mark, Luke and John *at least twice*. Make sure you understand everything Jesus did, regarding acts of love. We are not going to make it by understanding what the Apostle Paul alone wrote in the book of 1 Corinthians. We must do everything possible to learn how to love just like Jesus loved when he was on this earth, and the legacy of love he has left for us. We as men in the body of Christ must practice reading and practicing these tactics daily in order to show by example, our discipline and devotion to demonstrating love; the greatest spiritual self-defense tactic of all!

- Ask Christian friends and family members whose walk is true, to observe your practice, regarding mastering the "love tactic." Ask these people whether or not they believe you're on the right track, regarding the practice of and the expression of unconditional love.

Chapter 9

Things My Fifty-Five-Year-Old Self Wishes I Could Have Said to My Fourteen-Year-Old Self

How to Let Go of the Past, Move On, and Receive Your Healing

NOT TOO LONG AGO, I had the opportunity to take a look at my past. I was surfing the internet, when I decided to take a look at YouTube. I sometimes find it fun to "dream build" via YouTube, seeing places I've always wanted to visit, seeing successful people who are in a position where I want to be regarding my career aspirations, and seeing areas where I wouldn't mind living. Also, I like to reminisce by looking at video related to the Cincinnati I grew up knowing and loving: videos of the Coney Island and Kings Island amusement parks, the 1970s Big Red Machine Cincinnati Reds, and my hometown of Glendale, a small village about sixteen miles north of downtown. One day, I decided to look up an old 1979 Halloween special filmed in Glendale, a made-for-TV special in which I was an extra. Much to my surprise and excitement, I found the footage. I fast forwarded to the scene in which I could see myself riding my bicycle around Glendale's Village Square, the main center of town containing the shops and restaurants. The area's businesses are built around a circular area in which a beautiful fountain surrounded by an elevated garden sits. There I was, a slim, trim fourteen-year-old riding my Schwinn ten-speed bike around the square with two other neighborhood kids. I remember riding my bike around pretty fast, because I wanted to be seen as many times on TV as possible! As I was viewing my younger, much slimmer self, I felt compelled to pause the video, and zoom in on my image. As I looked at my likeness, I remembered the mistakes I made when I was that age. I made some mistakes that were serious ones, mainly of the reckless, life-threatening or juvenile delinquent-type. My friends and I used to hop slow-moving trains, hitching a ride to a nearby mall. We used to climb up the houses of neighborhood females who we thought were attractive, hoping to "sneak a peek" while they were undressing. We were like those guys in the film *Porky's* who snuck peeks in the high school girls' shower (yes, we did that too, peeking through a hole in a wall that led to the girls locker room). Several months from that summer day, we would plan and execute a robbery of a local Holiday Inn Holidome's video arcade. Just in case you've never seen one, back in the day, Holidomes were Holiday Inn's indoor mini-resorts, complete with an indoor pool and recreation area with putt-putt golf and other amenities. Also, when it came to area hotels like the Holidome, my friends and I were the biggest criminal trespassers, always sneaking in to go swimming, or get to know the female guests in our age range.

When I think about the fact that the things I did could've gotten me killed or arrested, I sometimes struggle with "what if" feelings about things that never happened. I could've slipped from the side of the train, falling under the train, something I especially feel guilty about. I could've gotten shot by a homeowner or a police officer. I could've had a criminal record. Also, even though you could call it a "boys will be boys" thing, I struggle with embarrassment, regarding thinking the stealing and "peeking." I'm thankful to say that at fifty-four years of age, I am still here, and I've never had a criminal record. About two years later, when I rededicated my life to the Lord, I stopped hopping trains, stealing quarters from video arcade machines, and criminal trespassing. I quit while I was ahead, thank the Lord God! Again, I thank the Lord God; the Lord God the Father, the Lord God the Son, and the Lord God the Holy Spirit for saving me before something tragic occurred. Still, as I looked at that still image of me, I wish that the fifty-four-year-old could go back in time and warn my fourteen-year-old self what *not* to do. However, I am thankful about many things in which the Lord has blessed me, with his protection coming to mind. I also thank the Lord God for blessing me with brothers and sisters in the body of Christ who have reminded me of the Lord God's protection for my life, even during those times when I had drifted away from having a relationship with him. I am happy to say that over the years, I have gotten much better, regarding dealing with this sort of thing. The more I have continued to work on my relationship with the Lord God, those personal feelings of guilt and embarrassment have lessened. I have learned through studying the Bible, that I am not condemned by the Lord God for the past things I've done because I belong to the Lord (Rom 8:1). I am thankful that the Lord loves me unconditionally, and that he loves me so much that he took my sins and all the guilt and shame associated with them, and tossed them into the sea of forgetfulness (Micah 7:19). Because of the importance of fellowship with other Christian men though the Victorious Men's Weapons for Warfare Bible Study at Williams Chapel AME Church, we have discussed the things about our past that have held us from stepping into every great thing the Lord has for us.

I bring up this very point because I believe that too many men are missing out on the blessings that the Lord wants them to experience. I believe this happens because many of them don't know who they really are in the body of Christ. Although they are believers, many don't know and understand the truth of what the Lord God says about them. I've brought this sort of thing up in the Bible study. I run the Bible study, and, as I mentioned previously I continue to notice that not as many men as we've expected have not been attending Bible study as I have hoped would be the case.

This has been the case despite the fact that I and others, at the beginning and end of church service, have actually reminded the men of the church of the importance of coming to Bible study and growing in the Lord, and learning just what the Lord God says about them. After posing my question about many men's lack of attendance at church and Bible study, one of the brothers stated that many men, when they do attend church, don't hear messages directed toward them. Instead, they hear the pastor direct their sermon topics toward women's issues. I've stated my belief that many men allow their pride and ego to keep them from really seeking the kind of relationship that the Lord God wants all of his children to have; the kind of relationship where we are in total submission to him, seeking help in all areas of our lives. They have bought into the world's belief that a man is supposed to have a rough, invulnerable exterior, and is supposed to be a so-called "self-made man" who can solve his most challenging problems on his own. I believe that there are many men who are believers who still have not totally "bought into" the truth that Jesus' yoke is easy and his burden is light (Matt 11:30), and that he will answer as long as we knock at the door and ask him for it (Luke 11:9–10). Another brother mentioned that we as men must go outside the walls of the church and get the word out to other men about the good news of Jesus, introducing our Lord and Savior to those who don't know him, and reintroducing those prodigal sons who are saved but who have drifted away from his grace and mercy.

Maybe what my brothers in the Bible study have said are parts of the problem that has resulted in more men not attending church and Bible study. It is still something I ponder. I have seen meetings after church where the men in leadership are almost pleading for more male involvement in church ministries. There may be up to more than a dozen men of various ages sitting in the pews listening to the plea. However, when it's time for action, many of the men are not showing up. Perhaps the answer is bringing more ministering to the streets. When my wife and I still lived in Maryland, I received the opportunity to do this. About five years ago, when my wife and I were members of Empowerment Temple AME Church in Baltimore, I was a member of the men's ministry. Our pastor, Reverend Jamal Bryant, devised what he termed "hood invasions," where the men would go into the heart of inner-city Baltimore neighborhoods and speak to the men, encouraging them to accept Jesus Christ as their personal Lord and Savior if they had not already done so. We also encouraged them to attend our church. I have fond memories of doing this, because I finally was not engaging in any excuses that would convince me not to witness this way. Jesus said we are to go forth and teach all nations (Matt 28:19). This is something that I'm trying to discipline myself to do on a regular basis.

A few years ago, I was watching a DVD from Dr. Tony Evans's *Kingdom Man* series. I have used this and other series from Dr. Evans for my Victorious Men's Bible Study at church. Dr. Evans is the pastor of Oak Cliff Bible Fellowship in Dallas, Texas. In the DVD set, he was talking to a group of Christian men when he said something quite profound. He ran into a man in the community who was, at one time, attending his church. However, he stopped coming to church without any explanation. When Dr. Evans asked the man why he stopped coming, he replied that he "didn't want any man telling him what to do, especially God."[1] Also, I read an article that stated that many men won't come to church if their wife or girlfriend constantly edifies the pastor. The article went on to explain that when this occurs, the man feels that the pastor is a rival rather than an ally; a rival who knows more spiritually than he, and is, because of his influence on his wife or girlfriend, a rival and a threat. The same article actually contains this thought-provoking passage:

> According to Pastor Diego Mesa of Word Harvest Church, a man begins to resent ministers when "he realizes that he can't compete with the moral examples set forth by the spiritual leader in his wife's life." Pastor Michael Williams of Joy Tabernacle in Houston addresses this problem by instructing married women in his church to tell their husbands about the Gospel, and not

1. From Evans, *Kingdom Man* (DVD series).

about him. "Don't go home and talk about me because you'll make me a rival." Pastor Mack Timberlake Jr. of the Christian Faith Center in Creedmoor, North Carolina also strives to avoid alienating the husbands of women in his church. He believes that his congregation has gone from being overwhelmingly female to over half male in the past 15 years in part because he tells women to talk to their husbands about the church's message, rather than its messenger.[2]

I found that to be a sad situation upon realizing that there are men out there with this mind-set; men who don't realize that total submission to the Lord God is the answer to victorious living.

The more I live, the more I realize that we men in the body of Christ must step up our spiritual self-defense training. Too much is at stake. I believe that the biggest challenge many of us must overcome is the fretting over and regret of past mistakes. I cannot go back and forewarn my fourteen-year-old self of the mistakes I am going to commit. At the same time, I can realize this powerful tool that fortifies my self-defense training: the Lord God knew every mistake I was going to make, and every test I was going to have to endure so that once I came back to him, I would have a series of testimonies that I can share with others who may be going through something that the Lord had me overcome.

At the same time, I must emphasize that my improvement upon putting the past behind me has everything to do with working on improving my spiritual self-defense. The Bible says that since I've accepted Christ, I have become a new creature; so new to the point where all of the old things, the past things of my live have passed away, and that all things are now a great, new beginning (2 Cor 5:17). I'm convinced that many men are going about life the hard way. Many of them are trying to figure out life on their own, falsely thinking that they can handle the challenges by themselves. Sooner or later, someone has to let them know that they are not going to know true success, true peace, true and real victorious living until they are in relationship with the Lord God the Father

2. Carlson, "That Old-Time Religion," 15.

(your Father in heaven), the Lord God the Son (Jesus, whose shed blood saved us), and the Lord God the Holy Spirit (the wonderful friend, that comforting presence that shows us what to do and not to do, and reveals to us correct life choices); the most powerful force in the universe.

One weekend, I was standing in the kitchen. It was a Saturday morning. As I stood there cracking eggs and adding spices for breakfast while my wife was preparing sausage, I realized how blessed I am. Despite the challenges of daily life, the fact that the Lord God has blessed me with a wonderful wife, breath in my body, a roof over my head, more than enough to eat, and wonderful opportunities for increase had resulted in an overwhelming spirit of gratitude and praise. I shared this immediately with my wife, who agreed with me.

If there's one key thing that you get from this book, it should be this: some of the most power weapons of spiritual self-defense you must master are those of gratitude and praise. You can always find something to thank and praise the Lord God for. Think about it, and you will find something. No matter what situation you're in, once you realize this and claim it, you'll find that this will give Satan, your enemy, a nervous breakdown, and that's a good thing. Here's how this powerful weapon of spiritual self-defense also helps me with successfully putting my past to rest; the powerful weapon of gratitude and praise reminds me that the Lord God allowed me to get through the rough times in order to experience the times that reminds me to literally shout out all of the wonderful things in which I can thank and praise the Lord God: so many numerous things that as long as I keep my mind on them as the Apostle Paul instructed (Phil 4:8) I will continually be on the path to mastering spiritual self-defense and have a fulfilling, productive life.

Bryce Harper is a Major League baseball player for the Philadelphia Phillies. He is one of the best hitters in baseball; one of the top five in the entire league. When I've watched him hit the ball, especially when he hits a home run, he engages in a specific technique. Right before he sees a pitch he wants to hit, he "bears down" in the batter's box by bending his knees, crouches down to a lower stance, and places the majority of his weight on his back leg and foot before he moves his front leg and swings the bat. The result is that he is transferring his weight in such a way as to provide optimum power for hitting the ball. His hitting style reminds me of a boxer who quickly pauses to plant his feet and bend down to shift his body weight before throwing an effective punch. I've heard boxing analysts refer to this technique as "sitting down on their punches." I've seen boxers such as Keith "One Time" Thurman knock out his opponents by doing this. Just as Bryce Harper bends his knees, plants himself in the batter's box and rears back before hitting that home run, and Keith Thurman sits down on his punches before knocking out an opponent, we Christian men must master the spiritual self-defense technique of letting the past bury it's dead. The Lord makes it clear that this is the most powerful spiritual self-defense technique we must master. This technique frees us to be the most effective man in the Lord God's kingdom because we now focus on the present, regarding the work of the kingdom of the Lord God. The Bible makes it clear that once we are in Christ, one we have accepted Jesus as our personal Lord and Savior, we are new creatures, newly appointed men in the body of Christ. Our old way of doing things, that person we used to be and that we no longer are, is dead; the former self that has now literally passed away (2 Cor 5:17). Dr. Tony Evans emphasizes this principal: we men in the body of Christ must leave yesterday behind. He explains that if we don't let go of the bad stuff especially, hanging on to our mistakes will keep us from our destiny. He also explains that the devil will tie us to yesterday in order to keep us from moving forward.[3]

In addition, here's a powerful realization as well: when we bury our past and move forward, while the devil now has a nervous breakdown because we are doing this, we increase that nervous breakdown by not dwelling on our past, but *using* our past as a living testimony to how the Lord delivered us from past troubles; another important spiritual self-defense technique. When we initiate this powerful move, it puts into motion the important result of

---

3. From Evans, *Kingdom Man* (DVD series).

what the devil meant for evil, the Lord God means for good (Gen 50:19–20)! Instead, my fifty-four-year-old self has learned to move forward, letting the past bury the dead, and *choosing only to refer to the past as evidence of a living testimony of the Lord's deliverance, grace and mercy!* This is a powerful spiritual self-defense tactic, because it is the Lord God showing me that once I exercise the power of choice, and choose to totally submit to the Lord God's will and have the necessary faith to do so, I latch onto so much power, the power of the Lord God the Father, the Lord God the Son, and the Lord God the Holy Spirit that it fortifies me with the power to let go of the past, and move forward onto my the Lord God-given destiny! This results in a freedom, a joy, an access to the most powerful force in the universe, the power of our eternal, all-powerful, all-knowing, always-present Lord God who has already given us this power to resist and overcome Satan, our already-defeated enemy! Men of the Lord God, you now know that through these techniques of spiritual self-defense, you have power that you previously didn't know you have. Now that you know, access that power! Move on and fulfill your destiny, you mighty man of the body of Christ! You are now gaining the knowledge and the power of spiritual self-defense!

Here's your next assignment for mastering spiritual self-defense:

- Identify those things of your past that are upsetting to you. Write them down. Afterward look up these scriptures in the Bible; ones that are specifically for successfully dealing with past hurts.

Chapter 10

It's Your Butt, and You Can Haul Garbage in It If You Want To

Fighting the Spirit of Stubbornness, and Stepping into Practicing the Lord God's Truth for Your Life

I NEVER HAD THE chance to meet my mother-in-law, the late Ms. Geraldine White. I was told in no uncertain terms by my wife, Karen, that she was funny like her, and that she molded and shaped her life through love, sometimes tough love through stern discipline, and an uncanny way of teaching her to always do everything in decency and order, with excellence and a profound sense of purpose. Karen told me that her mother loved life, loved her family, and loved being that graceful gracious host in her home, who could cook up a storm, make you feel and home, and entertain you with her energy and her witty sayings.

Karen told me that although her mother was all of these things, she did not suffer fools lightly, nor did she take any foolishness from anyone. She was known to say that due to their behavior, certain devious, misguided people could "tear up hell with a teaspoon." Karen told me that when her mother saw others being stubborn or foolish, with the result of negativity crashing down onto their lives due to lack of basic common sense based on bad choices, she would always have a particular saying (here's the G-rated version): "It's your butt, and you haul garbage in it if you want to." I'm sure you can guess that's not what she actually said! I can still remember the day Karen told me that my mother-in-law would say that upon witnessing basic human lack of wisdom. Have you ever heard something that made you laugh so hard that tears, those bellyache laugh tears just mist up your eyes and just about roll down your cheeks? That's how hard I laughed that day. And when my wife said it, she said it with that African-American female head-shaking attitude delivery that I'll bet her mother did it that way too; that "I know I'm telling it like it is" attitude. I never got the chance to meet her. In 1981, she passed away of a terminal illness. Still, I am thankful that my wife has told me about her; how she had a unique and effective way of conveying wisdom through funny, yet powerfully effective sayings.

At the same time, once I caught my breath and stopped laughing, I thought about how profound a statement that really was. I had never heard a statement like that. Now surely, I had heard the "it's your butt" statement before, but that one usually applied to various situations, some that you knowingly or unknowingly created or didn't create for yourself. Yet this was different. My mother-in-law's statement was very clear: If you choose to make jacked-up decisions, you were going to experience jacked-up results.

I refer to my mother-in-law's words, because if there is one key stronghold I have seen many men in the body of Christ struggle with, it is the stronghold of stubbornness. I believe that this spirit of stubbornness comes due to the fact that so many men in the body of Christ, who are stubborn about not coming to church, Bible study or Sunday school, walk in this neglect because of biological and spiritual fatherlessness. I was blessed tremendously with the presence of my father in my house and in my life. My father was and still is a strong Christian man who always believed in and still believes in taking instruction from his Heavenly Father, the Lord God, and passing that spiritual knowledge on to me. I will always be thankful to him for blessing me with a strong father who taught me to seek him first in all of my actions.

At the same time, as I mentioned previously, I know that there are many men in the Lord God's kingdom who did not receive what I received. I am well aware of the large numbers of men in the Lord God's kingdom who grew up without the presence of their biological father. Either he was not in the home, not involved in their lives at all, or a combination of both. And with that, these men have struggled with issues of anger and not forgiving their fathers for not being around to teach them how to be men in the body of Christ.

I have found that there is a need for those of you who have been directly affected by fatherlessness to tie into the church and seek men who can be your spiritual fathers while forming a relationship and connecting to your Father God Almighty, the Creator of the universe who loves you, will not leave you nor forsake you, and who will guide you to what is true manhood in his kingdom. I learned of the importance of spiritual fatherhood as one of the first key healing remedies for the pain of fatherlessness through one of my spiritual fathers, Dr. Tony Evans:

> The church must be where a man is not only to receive instruction for his own personal growth, but also where he is to take that instruction and teaching and rehearse it with his family during the week. It is supposed to be the place to grow boys into men through spiritual parenting such as what Paul wrote to his own "true children" and "beloved son" in his letters to Timothy and to Titus (see 1 Timothy 1:2; 2 Timothy 1:2; Titus 1:4). What is missing for men in the church are spiritual fathers like the apostle Paul. Without spiritual fathers to set the thermometer, we have an assembly line turning out a feminized version of what it means to be a man and calling him "nice" and "helpful" rather than "strong" and "responsible." Even though Timothy and Titus were not Paul's biological children, he spoke to them and related to them as a father would to a son. It is bad enough if a young man does not have a biological father to mentor him and help him grow, but when there is no spiritual father as well,

> he is fatherless twice. When a boy or a man is fatherless
> twice, he doubly misses out on receiving the blessing that
> he needs in his life.[1]

This is the crucial point, another key element in learning and mastering spiritual self-defense that all men in the body of Christ must get right! We all must overcome the stronghold of stubbornness when it comes to not going to church on a regular basis, and when we're there, seek and be the best spiritual fathers *we* possibly can be. I continue to learn that we as men in the body of Christ must stop being stubborn about going to church. The Bible makes it very clear, regarding the importance of regularly attending a Bible-teaching, Bible-believing church that practices the Lord God's principles:

> And let us *not give up meeting together*, as some are in the
> habit of doing, but let us encourage one another—and all
> the more as you see the Day approaching. (Heb 10:25)

This scripture always reminds me of the importance of attending church so that I can grow spiritually; a key part of gaining additional information to be the best practitioner of spiritual self-defense I can be. It is also important that I seek the guidance of spiritual fathers I reference in Bible study and this book; powerful men in the kingdom of the Lord God, such as Dr. Tony Evans, Dr. Bill Winston, Dr. Edwin Louis Cole, Pastor Joel Osteen, and Pastors Alex and Stephen Kendrick. Brothers, I cannot emphasize enough the process of asking the Lord God to connect you to spiritual fathers in the church; the one that the Lord God will direct to you. The Holy Spirit will tell you who to watch and learn from, as long as you are practicing spiritual self-defense. Your spiritual life depends on it. If you have a negative spirit of stubbornness, putting off this life or death decision can result in your harming and actually delaying your process of learning spiritual self-defense. Remember that the Bible tells us that we don't struggle against flesh and blood but against principalities (Eph 6:12). Dr. Tony Evans reminds us that people are not our problem. We are up

1. Evans, *Kingdom Man*, 184–86.

against spiritual forces in what the Bible calls heavenly places, that are demonic principalities that engulf people who don't know any better, and in some cases, people who do know better. You know better. Or if you didn't know, now you know. There are areas that Satan's demons control that we must not go near. At the same time, if we are in a position where we are unable to steer clear of these people affected by these principalities (a coworker, for example), or if people who are engulfed in these areas come around us, we must use our spiritual self-defense to successfully deal with them. Now that you are reading this information, and you know better, you can do better. Don't let excuses keep you from tying into surrogate and spiritual fathers, those who are expert practitioners of spiritual self-defense who can mentor you and guide you, and teach you that "spiritual muscle memory" I referred to earlier.

In addition, I really want you to take the time to work on any spirit of stubbornness you have about not going to church and taking part in its various ministries. Another point I want you to consider is the fact that tomorrow is not promised. As I wrote this part of the book, I remember that almost three years ago, I sat in my home office in South Carolina; just a little over an hour from where a deranged, demon-possessed, misguided young male stepped into the Mother Emanuel African Methodist Episcopal Church in Charleston, South Carolina, killing nine innocent worshippers and wounding three of them. I think about how their pastor, Reverend Clemente Pinkney, a strong man in the faith, and as a state senator, a respected political leader, was gunned down. That same evening, at Williams Chapel AME Church, I was conducting a Bible study right around that same time. When I came home and saw the horrific news on television, my first thoughts went back to earlier that year. For a celebration of our twelfth wedding anniversary, my wife and I drove to Charleston to a popular restaurant. As we were driving down a street toward the restaurant, we drove right by Mother Emanuel AME Church. Since I was not from the Charleston area, I did not know about the significance of the church; this was the first time my wife and I saw it. However, being a member of the AME Church all my life, and knowing history when I saw it, I could tell that the church had been around for quite some time; since right after the Emancipation Proclamation, which was my initial guess. Upon driving past the church, I remember saying to my wife something like, "Wow, I had no idea that a historic AME church was right in the downtown area. We ought to drive down for one of their services one day."

My wife agreed with my statement. Upon driving by that church that January night, we had no idea that five months later, an unspeakable tragedy would thrust Emanuel AME Church into the international spotlight. I thought to myself, that however the Lord sees fit to bring me home to glory, I want to make sure I am serving him, and doing the right thing as a Christian man. Everyone in that church was doing the right thing; loving on a stranger they had no idea was about to kill and maim them. It upsets and angers me that nine saints were taken from this earth this way, but I am thankful that they were prepared to go to be with the Lord. I think about the gospel music song "I Want to Be Ready When Jesus Comes." At the same time, I want to be ready to see Jesus when the time comes.

That said, I am reminded that I must do the best I can to be the best growth-oriented man in the kingdom of the Lord God I possibly can be. I try to do that by being discipled by people, especially other men I know of whom the Lord is working through to guide me in the right direction, and I try to do the same for those I'm leading and discipling. I must say this: it's the best feeling when I get together with other men in the church, via our Victorious Men Bible Study, and we pray with and for one another, share or triumphs and our trials, and especially, grow in the Lord together. The age range of our Bible study consists of men ranging in age from ninety-nine to the late 30's. Our oldest member is who I refer to as our esteemed elder, a man by the name of Mr. Carl Kennerly. Brother Kennerly is a retired educator, a man who was a high school principal in the Orangeburg, South Carolina, School District for over fifty years. He was also a renowned local civil rights leader who marched all over the South with the Southern Christian Leadership Coalition for desegregating all public facilities. He also served his country proudly in the Second World War. There have been times where Brother Kennerly has told us about all of the trials related to racism he experienced, and the struggles related to it. He told us once how during the war, he and the other African American soldiers were one time forced to get off of a train and sit in the back so that German prisoners of war could sit in the forward seats. He also shared with us how the same German POW's could shop in the base commissary, when the African American soldiers were not allowed in the same area. He has also told us how countless numbers of his former students still to this very day will walk up to him upon seeing him around town and tell him how if it had not been for his guidance and discipline, they would've ended up either not amounting to much in life, or not being the achieving, well-adjusted, productive citizens that they are.

When I think about Brother Kennerly, who at ninety-nine years of age still has a hunger for growing as a Christian man, I am truly humbled. Here is a man who has and continues to live a full life, enjoying his children, grandchildren, and great-grandchildren, and just enjoying being a blessing to others like myself. He walks two miles every day, weather permitting. When I think of how the Lord has and continues to work through Brother Kennerly, and how many people the Lord has blessed through his life, what I see from his example makes me want to be the best practitioner of spiritual self-defense I can possibly be.

When it comes to our Bible study, I am thankful that a negative spirit of stubbornness regarding avoiding the importance of fellowship and discipleship is not present among us. At the same time, I know that as the Bible tells us, the harvest is plentiful, but the laborers are few (Matt 9:37). Also, the Bible tells us not to forsake the assembling of ourselves together (Heb 10:25). We brothers in the Victorious Men's Bible Study know this, but we realize that so many men in the kingdom of the Lord God don't know this, or don't practice it. We realize that there are many men out there who feel lost spiritually. Many of them realize that their Father, the Lord God, can and will fill that void, but they seem reluctant to trust an honest, God-fearing man in a Bible-teaching, Bible-believing church to properly lead them, be their spiritual father, and show them how to live victoriously. There are times when at church, I've seen younger brothers in the balcony area; young brothers in their twenties and thirties, who come to church sporadically and socially keep their distance. It's as though they know that they need the guidance and leadership that comes with trusting a man or men in the church who want to be their spiritual fathers, but since they've been disappointed by men in their lives before, mainly their non-present biological fathers, they seem reluctant to trust the men in the environment that they need the most. So what happens is that many come to church irregularly, staying at what they believe is a "safe" physical and emotional distance from the very same men who the Lord God has assigned to them. And when the men of the church talk to many of them and encourage them to come to Bible study and other opportunities of fellowship, they come once in a while, or not at all.

This spirit of stubbornness, that stems from a lack of knowledge, is all a part of this harvest of so many men in the body of Christ, many of them young men, with a fair share of older men reaching their "middle years" who are struggling to commit to forming a real relationship with the Lord God, Jesus, and the Holy Spirit through allowing themselves to be mentored and discipled by spiritual fathers; those like the men in our Bible study. And many of these same men, Christian men who are not doing what they're supposed to be doing, wonder why they are struggling in life in general.

I have learned through the years of my adult life a very powerful lesson: when the Lord God assigns me a spiritual father, I must not take that relationship for granted, and I must follow the advice of that man who the Lord God has assigned to me. I have learned that sometimes the assignment lasts for a short or long season, and sometimes for a lifetime. I thank the Lord God for all of the spiritual fathers in my life.

Brothers, if you're struggling with a spirit of stubbornness, I want you to combat it and beat it down with spiritual self-defense tactics. I want you to first remember that you are in a spiritual war, and since you're in this, you need to be able to identify the weapons you must use for every battle. First, I encourage you to read and understand the following scripture:

> I beg you that when I come I may not have to be as bold as I expect to be toward some people who think that we live by the standards of this world. For though we live in the world, we do not wage war as the world does. The weapons we fight with are not the weapons of the world. On the contrary, they have divine power to demolish strongholds. We demolish arguments and every pretension that sets itself up against the knowledge of the Lord God, and we take captive every thought to make it obedient to Christ. And we will be ready to punish every act of disobedience, once your obedience is complete. (2 Cor 10:2–6)

What are these weapons? The key weapon I am sharing with you is the power of the Bible, making sure you follow what it says and applying it to your life. Scripture, when properly applied, is a powerful weapon for your warfare; the warfare against the stubbornness and disobedience that separates us from the Lord God. You must understand that all throughout the Bible, there have been examples where people in the Lord God's kingdom suffered due to their stubbornness. The entire book of Judges is a key example in the Bible of the Lord God raising up mighty warriors who successfully fought in many battles to restore Israel and take it back from their enemies. In each instance, the Hebrew people lost control of their land due to their stubbornness and disobedience to the Lord God (Judg 2:19), and as a result, their enemies overpowered them and took control of their land. In order to teach the Hebrew people to turn from these nonproductive ways, the Lord God raised up courageous and righteous people such as Gideon and Shamgar, to fight and win wars for the Hebrew people and restore Israel (Judg 7:19–25; Judg 3:31). Understand that the Bible makes it clear that stubbornness comes from arrogance (Deut 1:43; Neh 9:16).[2]4 The

2. This information is from Rev. Dr. Caesar R. Richburg's sermon titled "How We Handle Life's Hurts," July 12, 2015, Williams Chapel AME Church,

Lord God makes it clear that a spirit of arrogance that creates a spirit of stubbornness, is not the way he operates, nor does he expects we in the kingdom to behave that way.

Therefore, here is how you apply spiritual self-defense to this area of your life. Take note of these instructions:

- Seek forgiveness and grace from the Lord God. Read 1 Chronicles 16:11.5

- Submit to the Lord God in worship and obedience. Read 2 Chronicles 30:8.6

- Return to a life of trust and dependence toward the Lord God. Read Hosea 12:6.7

- Understand that Christ's death provides the solution to our spiritual stubbornness. Read Colossians 1:21–22.8

- Realize that fellowship with other believers, including encouraging and warning one another, can prevent the hard hearts that come from spiritual stubbornness. Read Hebrews 3:13.9

Orangeburg, South Carolina.

Conclusion

I WROTE THIS BOOK so that Christian men could have a guideline for them to understand and win spiritual warfare, through training in spiritual self-defense. I once heard Dr. Bill Winston and Rev. John K. Jenkins preach that although the Bible tells us that no weapon formed against us shall prosper (Isa 54:17), the fact remains that that does not keep the weapon from being formed. It is true that we are fighting against an already-defeated enemy, yet we must train to constantly defend ourselves in order to decrease the amount of wounds we do receive in battle.

Brothers, you must understand the power of being a believer. Once you make the decision to believe in Jesus, that he is the Son of the Lord God, and that you can only get to the Lord God the Father through him, then not only will you be saved, but your entire household will be saved, too. The Bible makes it very clear in the book of Acts, chapter 16, that when a man makes this decision, then he has made an everlasting life investment for himself; one that affects his entire family. This truth begins in v. 16, when the Apostle Paul and Silas have been jailed for preaching the good news of Jesus Christ to the people of Macedonia, and exorcising a demonic spirit out of a slave girl, whose ability to predict the future made money for her master. After they were severely beaten by the authorities, they were imprisoned. Yet, despite this unfair situation, they are staying up late at night praising the Lord God and singing hymns. We know this to be the case because the Bible tells us that it is this praise party one night that resulted in their freedom:

> About midnight Paul and Silas were praying and singing hymns to the Lord God, and the other prisoners were listening to them. Suddenly there was such a violent earthquake that the foundations of the prison were shaken. At once all the prison doors flew open, and everybody's chains came loose. The jailer woke up, and when he saw the prison doors open, he drew his sword and was about to kill himself because he through the prisoners had escaped. Burt Paul shouted, "Don't harm yourself! We are all here!" The jailer called for lights, rushed in and fell trembling before Paul and Silas. He then brought them out and asked, "Sirs, what must I do to be saved?" They replied, "Believe in the Lord Jesus, and you will be saved—*you and your household.*" (Acts 16:25)

You see that this part of the scripture emphasizes this important fact: when a man makes up his mind to believe in Jesus and serve him, the family is positively affected from and benefits from this outcome. At the same time, the man, after seeing the miracle, and hearing the good news, must *choose* to believe in Jesus! Now speaking of good news, the jailer, upon witnessing the miracle, asking what he must do to be saved, and hearing what he must do, *made the decision* to do the right thing for him and his family:

> At that hour of the night the jailer took them and washed their wounds; *then immediately he and all his family were baptized.* The jailer brought them into his house and as-set a meal before them; he was filled with joy because *he had come to believe in the Lord God—he and his whole family.* (Acts 16:33–34)

Notice that the jailer saw that this was a life-or-death situation for him and his entire family; one that he handled right away. He knew that now, since the Lord worked through Paul and Silas to reveal the truth, when it came to the matter of his and his family's soul salvation, he knew better than to procrastinate. He knew that he had to use the Lord God's window of opportunity to lock down eternal life for himself and everybody in his household.

Now I understand that there may be those of you who say, "Well Brother Patrick, it was easier for this man to believe because he saw the Lord God's power when he shook the ground and opened the prison doors." Well that's the wrong way of looking at this situation. Hebrews 11:1 tells us that "faith is the substance of things hoped for, the evidence of things not seen." To me, that means that instead of seeing then believing, your faith in the Lord God and your relationship with him is first about believing, and then seeing! It is no coincidence that many twelve-step programs that help people with addictions have as a foundation one key step; that a person *comes to believe* that a power greater than themselves can restore them to sanity. So before a person is delivered from their addiction, they believe that they are delivered from it before they see it happen! We know that the power greater than ourselves is the Lord God—the Father, the Son, and the Holy Spirit! This is the foundation, the solid rock on which we stand! The Bible tells us that when you declare with your mouth that Jesus is Lord, and believe in your heart that the Lord God raised him from the dead, then you shall be saved (Rom 10:9).

So if you've already made this decision and you've asked the Lord to come into your life, and believe that Jesus Christ is the Son of the Lord God, your Savior, and that the Lord God raised him from the dead and you've repented of your sins, then you are on your way. At the same time, you must realize that even if you've made this decision now or some time ago, you must now realize that you need the tools of spiritual self-defense; the same tools that if applied, will show you how to win the battles of spiritual warfare. Since you believe, you've have the victory, but the Lord God the Father, the Lord God the Son, and the Lord God the Holy Spirit does not want you to live a miserable, strife-filled life because of lack of knowledge. We serve a loving Lord God who through his Son Jesus, wants you to have life, and have it more abundantly (John 10:10).

Remember that we are more than conquerors (Rom 8:37). Yet we must continue to love wisdom, stay in top spiritual shape, and always be ready to practice our spiritual self-defense skills. I would not have introduced these skills had I not tested them myself. Anytime I found myself in a situation where I had to exercise my Bible-based spiritual self-defense skills, as long as I exercised those skills, everything turned out the right way; the Lord God's way. We always want to put ourselves in a position to win, regarding our Christian walk. A good Christian friend said something to me that really struck me as profound: the Bible was not written for discussion, it was written for production. We must apply the spiritual self-defense techniques, and not just talk about them. Make sure you are applying what you've learned, practicing daily to be the best person you can be in the body of Christ. When you do this, it means that you are about your father's business; your Father in heaven. Work on being such a successful practitioner of spiritual self-defense to the point where you let your light shine so brightly that you attract others who want what *you* have.

Have I always been successful in applying spiritual self-defense techniques? No, I don't have a spotless track record, not by a long shot. I, just like any other Christian, is a work in progress. I just continue to pray and work at this spiritual walk. Every day, I seek to regroup and improve upon my techniques. I realize it is about winning spiritual warfare. It is about slaying the flesh, and doing what the Holy Spirit tells us to do. The most successful warriors of antiquity survived battles and conquered their enemies not only because they sharpened their skills to a knife edge, and studied each battleground; they were also acutely aware of their surroundings at all times, ready to react correctly at a moment's notice. In his book *World War Me: How to Win the War I Lost*, Dr. Jamal Bryant stresses that since we in the body of Christ are always immersed in spiritual warfare, we must constantly be in training. He reminds us that the Lord God always requires Christians to train daily for the battle against an already-defeated enemy. Remember: although the Bible tells us that no weapon formed against us shall prosper, that does not mean that the weapon is not going to be formed in the first place. We must make sure that we are training daily, regarding our spiritual self-defense tactics. I encourage you to read Rev. Dr. Bryant's book, and other books that prepare you, regarding your spiritual self-defense. Other great books are Joyce Meyer's *Battlefield of the Mind: Winning the Battle in Your Mind*; Dr. John Maxwell's *Running with the Giants*; Rev. Larry Lea's *Weapons of Your Warfare: Equipping Yourself to Defeat the Enemy*, and any book I have previously mentioned.

Why is it important for us to read and tie into the examples I've just mentioned? As men in the body of Christ, we must make a decision to hold onto and live by the truth, no matter what the consequences. There is a truth that is in the Bible, a truth that the Lord God wants you to know about him, his risen Son, Jesus, and the Holy Spirit, the Spirit of Truth that he designed to guide you. We must walk in truth, brothers, because if we don't do this, we are living a lie and destined to fail. What do I mean by that? Here's what I mean: If you are not living by the truth that is the Word of the Lord God, and not walking in the Spirit or speaking what the Lord God says about you, and not adhering to and following his instruction in the form of doing what the Lord God the Father, the Lord God the Son, and the Lord God the Holy Spirit instruct, then you are flying blind. You are playing with fire. You are engaging in spiritual Russian roulette, and that's a game you will lose! We cannot play with this, brothers! We are in a war! Spiritual warfare is real, and we must prepare for a daily battle! The truth is that we are supposed to love our neighbors as ourselves (Mark 12:31). The truth is that we are supposed to be kind to other human beings, and love them just like the Lord loves us (Eph 4:31). The truth is that we are supposed to be men of honor who do not constantly fight each other, disrespect each other, nor engage in deadly confrontations with each other (Matt 7:12). Do the opposite, and allow the enemy to use you, which is the stupidest thing you or any other man in the body of Christ can do. Don't fall for the enemy's okeydoke! He is not creative, and will use the same old played-out tricks to sucker you in! You have to decide right here and now that you have had enough of his foolishness, and that you are better than his petty little stupid time-wasting tricks! We are men now, and a man does not engage in the childish, immature, knuckle-headed stuff that the enemy wants us to do! Either we are going to be men in the body of Christ, live by the Lord God's word, his guidance, and his principles, or be mental boys who let the enemy push us around, jacking up our spiritual and family relationships. I'm not letting that happen. I've drawn a line in the sand, and I've chosen the former; for the Lord God I live, and for the Lord God I will die! That is victorious living! You ought to make the same choice, too! This is what a *real man* does!

In my work office, I have a Palm Sunday palm leaf fashioned in the shape of a cross, hanging on my office wall. There are times when I'm driving, and although I'm listing to Christian music on my radio, I still am going through spiritual warfare. There are times when I'm driving, for example, and the craziness associated with dealing with reckless drivers around me makes my flesh rise up in me. Sometimes I feel like allowing the flesh to take over, but I remain calm and say a prayer (sometimes the prayer is one of asking the Lord to forgive me for my corrupt communication!). Yes, I catch a grip and remember my spiritual self-defense train-ing, because in order for me to act right, I must always do this, for to do so is to receive and believe the good news that is the risen Christ. I do this so I will never forget what Jesus did for me, the unimaginable suffering on that cross, that horrible suffering he went through for my sins. I will never forget that he took my place on that cross. I must never forget his sacrifice to me. When I hold onto Jesus' goodness, I practice spiritual self-defense and I hold onto my common sense. I hold onto the hope that is in my hands, because through my risen Savior, just like that old gospel music song says: because he lives, I can face tomorrow. I must always look to the cross, because I realize that as long as I do that, I will make the right decisions, and I will do the right thing. I struggle at times just like any other man in the body of Christ, but I hold onto the hope that is my faith. I believe that no matter how challeng-ing things become, I hold onto the promise of what the Bible says about me: I stand on those promises. I believe that I am fearfully and wonderfully made (Ps 139:14)! I believe that the Lord God that is inside me is greater than this no-good flesh that I struggle with and against daily (1 John 4:4).

When you really think about it, brothers, at the end of the day, what we really want is peace of mind. What we have to realize is that the true peace of mind comes through having a real relationship with the Prince of Peace, so that we can have that perfect peace, the peace that goes beyond all understanding. One key thing we must do is realize that as Christian men, we have work to do; we don't have time to mess around. We don't have time to get caught up in the foolishness of the world, for the world will try to veer our attention from spiritual things, the work of the Lord God the Father, the Lord God the Son, and the Lord God the Holy Spirit; whatever is not of this is of the world, that stuff we must not focus our attention on. We have to renew our minds (Rom 12:2) because we have too much work to do in the body of Christ, and that's a good thing; that's a good place to be in which we must focus our attention. The Apostle Paul reminded us to think about things that are pure, lovely, admirable, excellent and praiseworthy (Phil 4:8).

During the time my wife and I still lived in Maryland, while attending a March 2011 marriage retreat sponsored by our church, I was blessed in a major way by Bishop Clifford and co-pastor Pamela Frazier, of the City of Life Christian Church, in St. Louis, Missouri. Married for thirty-seven years, their ministry, Battle for the Family,[1] is designed to enrich through Christian leadership and education, all families in the body of Christ. Our church was blessed through their leadership, regarding our church's marriage ministry, who invited them to work with the church's married couples. On the second day and second half of the marriage retreat, Bishop and First Lady Frazier divided the grouping into the men, who met with the bishop, and the women, who met with the first lady. Bishop Frazier led us (the men) into a separate room so he could engage us in some real talk, regarding how men in the body of Christ are really supposed to handle their business. He

---

1. See http://www.battleforthefamily.com/v3/.

didn't sugarcoat it. He let us know point blank that we as Christian men are commanded *to lead, take charge, and accept responsibility.* He made it crystal clear that the man is responsible for setting the spiritual atmosphere of the household, and that the Lord God is seeking accountability on our part. Bishop Frazier encouraged us to read the fifty-fourth chapter of Isaiah, and take note of the courageous men who did the Lord God's will. I remembered Bishop Frazier's words, and I thank the Lord God for introducing me to another spiritual father in my life. I have applied his advice, and I've been able to add that as a powerful weapon, regarding my spiritual self-defense arsenal.

Stay strong in the Lord, my brother! You are a strong man of the Lord God, and you *will* earn your black belt in spiritual self-defense!

Bibliography

Beers, Gilbert, and Ronald Beers. *Touch Points for Men: the Lord God's Answers to Your Daily Needs.* Carol Stream, IL: Tyndale, 1998.

Carlson, Tucker. "That Old-Time Religion: Why Black Men Are Returning to Church." *Policy Review* 61 (1992) 13–17.

Carnegie, Dale. *How to Stop Worrying and Start Living.* New York: Simon & Schuster, 1944.

Chapman, Gary. *The Five Love Languages: How to Express Heartfelt Commitment to Your Mate.* Chicago: Northfield, 1992.

Evans, Tony. *Kingdom Man.* Colorado Springs: Focus on the Family, 2015.

Fondacaro, Karen M., et al. "Psychological Impact of Childhood Sexual Abuse on Male Inmates: The Importance of Perception." *Child Abuse & Neglect* 23 (1999) 361–69.

Kendrick, Alex, and Stephen Kendrick. *The Love Dare.* Paris, ON: B&H, 2008.

Kunjufu, Jawanza. *Developing Positive Self-Images and Discipline in Black Children.* Chicago: African American Images, 1984.

Maltby, John. "Church Attendance and Anxiety Change." *Journal of Social Psychology* 138 (1998) 537–38.

McCall, Nathan. *Makes Me Wanna Holler: A Young Black Man in America.* New York: Vintage, 1995.

Shakespeare, William. *The Merchant of Venice.* In *The Complete Pelican Shakespeare*, edited by Stephen Orgel and A. R. Braunmuller, 285–323. New York: Penguin, 2002.

Wilkinson, Bruce. *Secrets of the Vine: Breaking Through to Abundance.* Sisters, OR: Multnomah, 2006.

Wilson, Eric, et al. *Fireproof.* Nashville: Nelson, 2008.

Winston, Bill. *The Law of Confession: Revolutionize Your Life and Rewrite Your Future with the Power of Words.* Tulsa, OK: Harrison, 2009.

www.ingramcontent.com/pod-product-compliance
Lightning Source LLC
Chambersburg PA
CBHW070508090426
42735CB00012B/2695